A Wrestle
Before God

LATTER-DAY SAINT
THEOLOGY SEMINAR

THE LATTER-DAY SAINT THEOLOGY SEMINAR is based on a novel idea: that Latter-day Saints do theology. Doing theology is different from weighing history or deciding doctrine. Theology experiments with questions and advances hypotheses. It tests new angles and pulls loose threads.

To this end, the Seminar organizes interdisciplinary, collaborative, theological readings of Latter-day Saint scripture. Seminar participants with diverse backgrounds closely explore familiar texts in creative ways. In frequent partnership with the Laura F. Willes Center for Book of Mormon Studies at the Neal A. Maxwell Institute for Religious Scholarship at Brigham Young University, the Latter-day Saint Theology Seminar presents these experiments upon the word to foster greater theological engagement with basic Restoration texts.

A Wrestle Before God

Reading Enos 1

Edited by
Adam S. Miller

LATTER-DAY SAINT
THEOLOGY SEMINAR

Contents

Introduction

Adam S. Miller

Co-sponsored by the Latter-day Saint Theology Seminar and Brigham Young University's Neal A. Maxwell Institute for Religious Studies, together with funding from Laura F. Willes Center for Book of Mormon Studies, the 2022 theology seminar, "A Wrestle Before God: Reading Enos 1," was held at Columbia University in New York City from June 19 to July 1, 2022.

As in the past, the seminar's directors and six participants worked for two weeks on the text, Enos 1:1–18. These eighteen verses in Enos constitute an extraordinarily rich and deeply personal text about Enos's own "wrestle" with God as he sought forgiveness for his sins and then, in turn, pled for the future of his own people and his brothers, the Lamanites.

The first week of the seminar was dedicated to generating close, collaborative readings of the text, treating just three or four assigned verses each day. Seminar participants focused each morning on writing a short, formal paper on the day's assigned verses. They then spent five hours each afternoon collectively discussing the details and implications of the day's verses and sharing the formal work they'd prepared that morning. This first week of seminar-style work is extremely intense, with participants often working ten to twelve hours a day to prepare for and then participate in the day's collaborative work.

The second week of the seminar then centered on writing individual papers, grounded in that first week's shared work, to be presented at a public conference on the seminar's final day. Participants drafted full conference papers in less than three days, workshopped those papers on Wednesday, and then presented polished drafts at the conference on Friday. Those conference papers are collected here in this volume of the Latter-day Saint Theology Seminar's proceedings.

When we began organizing the seminar in 2008, we had a vision of what the project might accomplish over the coming decades. That vision turned on the conviction that, as a long-term project, the value of these seminars would be compounding, with each new seminar expanding the community of scholars who had participated and with each new volume of proceedings deepening the value of the publications that had preceded it. With more than a decade's worth of work under our belt, we believe this vision is proving true. We're grateful for all those who have participated and for those whose generous support has made this work possible.

Enos as Every-body

Sharon J. Harris

EVERYBODY LOVES ENOS. His account is broadly relatable enough to appeal to many different people and individual enough that readers feel that the story is meaningful to them personally. Enos is accessible and seems to be a "regular" person. He flattens hierarchy that we might feel from prophets, priests, kings, and typical record keepers. He tells how he wrestled, and God answered. In short, Enos is an Everyman. Conveniently, the name "Enos" means "mortal" and "man," and is thus like a Hebrew version of "Everyman."[1] By generalizing Enos this way, the name turns Enos's character into a kind of open role for anyone to fill. In the spirit of this broad applicability, I use the term Everybody instead of Everyman. Today I offer speculative thoughts on what we find if we think of the Book of Enos as an Every-body text. This approach to Enos offers an explanation for some of the difficulties and questions within the text. It also opens possibilities to think of the story of Enos as an oral text—recited, heard, and possibly enacted. As an

---

1. Like his Biblical precedent Enos, the son of Seth, Enos in the Book of Mormon is the first generation not part of a founding family, whether Adam and Eve and their children, or Lehi and Sariah and their children. As such, in both families Enos is the position of making his way separated from inaugural covenant events and *in absentia* from God, relying on his peers to teach and walk with him. It is appropriate, then, that in the Book of Mormon, Enos is an icon of prayer, raising his voice from earth "high that it reached the heavens" (4).

1

oral, Every-body text, the book of Enos invites identification with it and mimesis of it. We can speculate on how it could be deployed, enacted, or even ritualized. Speculating on Enos as an Every-body text, we can try to understand why everybody loves Enos.

1. Questions about Enos

First, I turn to some of the challenges in the Enos text. If we take the dates given in the books of Jacob, Enos, and Jarom seriously, it gets complicated. How old was Jacob when he received the plates after Nephi died? He must have been at least middle-aged, perhaps older. Enos says he was taught by his father, indicating that their lives overlapped long enough for Enos to have received these lessons. It is possible that Enos lived at least a bit longer after he closed the record as well. The only record between the beginning of Jacob's and the beginning of Jarom's books is Enos. It presents itself as representing a single generation, but it is a generation that lasts for 145 years. The amount of time covered by Enos's record stretches credulity.

For a book of scripture that culminates in the promise of a record to come forth, the text of Enos covered in this theology seminar, verses 1–18, is far less invested in its own status as a record, especially a written record.[2] All other entries in the small plates section of the Book of Mormon foreground their provenance and transmission as a written account of the Lehites. Most of the writers do this at the beginning and end of each entry so much so that it is formulaic: Nephi says, "I, Nephi, wrote this record" and finishes, "I have been commanded of him to write these things" (1 Ne. heading; 2 Ne. 33:11). Jacob opens and closes, "he gave me, Jacob, a commandment that I should write upon these plates" and "I make an end of my writing upon these plates" (Jacob 1:2; 7:27). All the other writers of the small plates—Jarom, Omni, Amaron, Chemish, Abinadom, and Amaleki—say something about writing the record. In the case of Chemish, that's about all he said. But

---

2. Enos 1:19–27, not studied in our seminar, seem to function differently from the self-contained account of prayer in the first eighteen verses and I do not include them in my analysis of Enos as an Every-body text.

not Enos. We can imagine a recordkeeper noticing the several years between Jacob and Jarom, picking up on the name "Enos" left at the end of Jacob's record, which might also have just meant, "the guy," and deciding to insert what may have been a popular, informal account of the Lehite covenant in the form of a personal story.

The speaker's nondescript name as well as a lack of names in the Enos text also raise questions. Enos's name sets up the book to be read as an Every-body story, as we have seen. Enos also speaks of "my father" at some length, but, conspicuously, the father is not named. Perhaps the father is Jacob, but this is left unspecified, inviting anyone who takes up the text to imagine their own father in the paternal role. The text holds open a space for the psychological impact of fathers but keeps it generic so that anyone can put themselves in Enos's or Every-body's shoes. Even Enos's mode of self-identification works this way. When Enos says, "I, Enos," four times, the doubled self-reference—first "I," followed by the name—simultaneously performs the particular and the general. The "I" invites the speaker of the story to take up the first-person position, and the name "Enos" locates that "I" in the broad, basic category of mortal humans.

Every-body characteristics of the Book of Enos show how it generalizes and particularizes. Both its generality and its particularity render it more available and highlight how it can work as an Every-body text. The text depersonalizes its names, dates, and transmission, and it does this itself, rather than through the editorial hands that shape so much of the Book of Mormon. Even the details about Enos hunting in the forests expand the possibilities of whom we can see in the text. The Lamanites are consistently portrayed as those who eat beasts and hunt, in contrast to the agrarian Nephites.[3] And the Book of Mormon mentions forests only in the land of Nephi, which is primarily the home of the Lamanites. Might the story of Enos evoke images of a Lamanite hunting in forests? Whether Lamanite or Nephite, it is not evident that Enos is of a high social class or even fully integrated in society as he wanders alone, reckoning with his father's teachings. Perhaps this is a narrative meant to apply to a wide swath of Lehites, not just Nephites.

---

3. See 2 Ne. 5:11, 24; Enos 1:20; and Jarom 1:6.

The ways that the Book of Enos is scrubbed of specifics makes it more widely relatable, but so, too, do the specifics it includes. It occludes details that might pinpoint it to a moment or an individual in history in favor of presenting a repeatable story. While the Enos text presents a general story of seeking God, it particularizes its language. One of the appeals of the account is how Enos feels chatty and accessible. He begins conventionally, "Behold, it came to pass," but quickly discards the formality for side notes, interjections, and unfinished phrases.[4] Enos's approachable unpretentiousness adds to the Every-body feel. As already seen, the Book of Enos distances itself from historical recordkeeping more than any other entry on the small plates. Instead of foregrounding a kind of social, religious, or archival status, it appeals to the individual experience of soul-hunger. It relates an experience of yearning and struggle that is at once deeply personal and widespread. This is Enos, the mortal, the Every-body we can imitate. He holds out the ideal of turning from our own cares to concern for others. The culmination of his wrestle offers the possibility that we, too, can secure a covenant from God. In this way, Enos is cousin to a text like Job. Rather than prioritizing history, the book of Job transcends time to tell the story of one man's struggle with God. Likewise, Enos's wrestle is like the frame story of Job that Robert Alter says "in all likelihood [is] a folktale that had been in circulation for centuries, probably through oral transmission."[5]

What happens if we think of the book of Enos as an oral text? The text itself emphasizes aurality. Enos remembers the words he *heard* his father speak, and he describes his prayer as crying and raising his "voice high that it reached the heavens" (4). Likewise, the answers to his prayers are often aural. He says, "there came a voice unto me," "when I had heard these words," and "after I, Enos, had heard these words" (5, 9, 11).[6] The Enos text contains multiple allusions to the Psalms, as

---

4. After the opening phrase, the rest of verse one is a series of these digressions. Verse 2 cuts off the ending thought of verse 1.

5. Robert Alter, Introduction to Job in *The Wisdom Books: Job, Proverbs, and Ecclesiastes*, trans. Robert Alter (New York: W. W. Norton, 2010), 4.

6. A variant to these examples is verse 10, "the voice of the Lord came into my mind again."

Kylie Turley has demonstrated in our conversations at the seminar, and Psalms are explicitly oral—they are sung prayers, often performed in liturgical settings. The world of Enos is full of sounds and voices, and, in contrast to much of the rest of the Book of Mormon, it is a personal story more than a history or sermon. It lends itself to telling and retelling, to oral culture. Oral transmission means that a text is reworked, revised, and recycled in the mouths of multiple tellers. Across these several narrators, the tale crosses time and communities. Its reuse testifies to its wide appeal and also ensures that it will stay relevant as it is retold to new listeners.

2. Enos Enacted

Retelling a text imbues it with ahistorical fable-like qualities. What changes again if it is not only told but also performed? In fifteenth-century England, the Everyman story of salvation was developed into a play. Salvation could be enacted. In this next section, I consider echoes of Enos told and enacted within the Book of Mormon as well as how the text invites us to understand it as enactable.

When something is performed, it is enacted within a *mise en scène*, which simply means the setting and arrangement of the physical surroundings. The forest is the setting of Enos's record. As noted, in the Book of Mormon forests are called such only in the land of Nephi. For most of the Book of Mormon, the land of Nephi is where the Lamanites live. But, 200 years after Enos's record, another group of Nephites emphasized a sylvan environment in the land of Nephi. The account of Alma's founding of a church highlights the physical surroundings where it occurred: "all this was done in Mormon, yea, by the waters of Mormon, in the forest that was near the waters of Mormon; yea, the place of Mormon, the waters of Mormon, the forest of Mormon, how beautiful are they to the eyes of them who there came to the knowledge of their Redeemer" (Mosiah 18:30). Some verses earlier Mormon explains the source of this name (which is also his name), that there was "a place which was called Mormon, having received its name from the king, being in the borders of the land having been infested, by times or at seasons, by wild beasts" (Mosiah 18:4). Years later in Zarahemla

Alma$_1$ receives a response to a prayer that refers to "they who were baptized in the waters of Mormon" (Mosiah 26:15). In these examples the physical space of the founding of the Lehite church comes forward. This space and Enos's *mise en scène* share the similarities of forests and beasts. Not only are the settings similar, however; in both cases the narrators of these accounts draw attention to the setting. Is Mormon, the editor-in-chief, foregrounding forests and beasts in the land of Mormon in order to link the secret conversion of Alma's followers to Enos's forest prayer? The outdoor wild settings mark these narratives as set apart from normal life. The greenspace frame heightens the mystical and vulnerable sense of these stories, that anything could happen in the woods.

If the story of Enos comes from an oral tradition and is told like a tale, its setting makes it more like a fairytale that takes place in a liminal, magical space. If it is performed, the setting signals the performance, that something designated and deliberate is being done outside the routines of regular living and action. Joseph Smith went to a grove. Nephi went to a mountain. Enos went to a forest. These were not enacted performances taking on the role of someone else, but removal to a specific setting can have the effect of the first stage direction of a script. It opens the way to make what follows performative.

Besides the physical setting, what if the Enos-text was seen as a kind of Lehite script for the performance of conversion, prayer, and covenant? If it was orally transmitted, the words would have been familiar, living, as they say, rent-free in people's minds. We can hear these echoes of Enos throughout the Book of Mormon. First, in narratives of conversion: when Alma$_1$ invited his followers to be baptized, he said,

> Behold, here are the waters of Mormon (for thus were they called) and now, as ye are desirous to come into the fold of God, . . . that ye may have eternal life—Now I say unto you, if this be the desire of your hearts, what have you against being baptized in the name of the Lord, as a witness before him that ye have entered into a covenant with him, that ye will serve him and keep his

commandments, that he may pour out his Spirit more abundantly upon you? (Mosiah 18:8–10)

Alma₁ emphasized the "desire of [their] hearts," eternal life, making a covenant with the Lord, keeping commandments, and pouring out the Spirit.

Each of these images and ideas are also in the book of Enos. Enos talks of his desire (9, 12–13), the words of his father "concerning eternal life" (3), the covenant God made with him (16), the contingency of Nephite blessing on their keeping commandments (10), of pouring out his "whole soul" (9), and of spirit (10). In particular, Enos lays out his desire multiple times. First he relates the desire he felt "for the welfare of [his] brethren," and the Lord responds explicitly to Enos's desires, answering, "I will grant unto thee according to thy desires" (9, 12). Enos introduces his lengthy, final-draft desire by saying, "And now behold, this was the desire which I desired of him" (13). An echo of this resonates in the response to Alma's invitation, "And now when the people had heard these words, they clapped their hands for joy [also found in Enos], and exclaimed, 'This is the desire of our hearts'" (Mosiah 18:11).

Might the Enos tale have been a model for conversion, one they could call on when they enacted their own conversion at the waters of Mormon? In addition to stating their desire explicitly, their response is not just stated but performed, complete with joy, hand clapping, and exclamation. In other conversion narratives, the people of King Benjamin fell down when they heard his words, not unlike Enos kneeling down in his wrestle. Ammon looked like Enos when he "fell upon his knees, and began to pour out his soul" (Alma 19:14). King Lamoni, the queen, and Ammon all sink down in the joy and overwhelm of their conversion, with joy and sinking as additional images from Enos (3). Perhaps they knew of a precedent of falling down and communing with God from a circulating folktale of Enos, making it easier to know what to do when they found themselves in an analogous position.

Several Book of Mormon accounts echo Enos's prayers. Limhi's people cry "all the day long," the same descriptor found in Enos (Mosiah 21:14). Amulek instructs the Zoramites on how to pray with directions that reverberate of Enos: "ye must pour out your souls in your closets, and your secret places, and in your wilderness." Amulek goes on to say that even when not crying to the Lord, your hearts should be "drawn out continually for your welfare, and also for the welfare of those around you" (Alma 34:26–27). In a tragic quotation of Enos, Mormon tells how he loved the Nephites "and my soul had been poured out in prayer unto my God all the day long for them" but, in contrast to Enos, "it was without faith" because he knows God will bring down their transgressions on their heads (Mormon 3:12). I do not analyze the parallels between the prayers of Enos and the brother of Jared here, but Moroni's account draws many similarities. Both are portrayed as unsure and struggling through several questions. Both deal with a fractured society. Both stories emphasize language. Both pray at length and have a dialogue with God. They express their confusion and ask questions. In response to their questions, both are told, "because of thy faith" (Enos 1:12 and Ether 3:9). After Enos's prayer, many prayers that follow in the Book of Mormon look like asking questions, going to secret places, pouring out one's soul, and crying to the Lord all the day long. They look a lot like Enos.

Enos as an Every-body text also offers a model for covenanting. When Alma₁ founded the church, he invited the people to covenant. When Captain Moroni initiated a covenant among the Nephites around the title of liberty, he was thinking of the Lord's promises regarding the Nephites as told to Enos:

> I will visit thy brethren according to their diligence in keeping my commandments. I have given unto them this land, and it is a holy land; and I curse it not save it be for the cause of iniquity; wherefore, I will visit thy brethren according as I have said; and their transgressions will I bring down with sorrow upon their own heads (10).

With this as backdrop, we can look at how Captain Moroni "poured out his soul to God" and then named the land the "land of liberty," like the holy land mentioned in Enos (Alma 46:17 and Enos 1:10). Moroni reasoned, "Surely God shall not suffer that we, who are despised because we take upon us the name of Christ, shall be trodden down and destroyed, until we bring it upon us by our own transgressions" (Alma 46:17–18). In this same vein, Helaman later worried that the "judgments of God should come upon our land, to our overthrow and utter destruction" (Alma 58:9–10). He may have been thinking of the Lord's instructions to Enos. If the Enos text diagnosed the problem Helaman feared, it also offered a response. Helaman explained, "*Therefore* we did pour out our souls in prayer to God, that he would strengthen us and deliver us out of the hands of our enemies, yea, and also give us strength that we might retain our cities and our lands" (Alma 58:9–10, italics added). Helaman took up Enos-like prayer to forestall the destruction of the Nephites and try to keep their lands. The story of Enos is an individual, enactable account of Lehite salvation in miniature. If Enos is an Every-body narrative, and he secured a covenant from the Lord that a record would be preserved and eventually help bring a Lehite remnant back to the covenant of Israel, then, presumably, any Lehite could enact the same prayer and process and remake this covenant.

But not just Lehites. Modern readers have turned to the book of Enos as a template for religious exercises. For decades various teachers—from religion instructors at BYU to youth Sunday school teachers in local wards—have encouraged students to have a "long prayer like Enos" with varying degrees of success.[7] One student from the 2010s recalls feeling that God was humoring the prayer. Another from the 1970s reports that the attempt was a "complete failure."[8] A seminary teacher says she "especially and repeatedly" listened to the LDS seminary song based on Enos called "My Soul Hungered."[9] LDS missionaries have used the story of Enos in trainings and as designated scripture study.[10] One returned missionary recounts that her mission president asked them to read the book of Enos every day for a month and communicate each week via letter what they had learned. In an oral history, one person tells that in pre-1978 Ghana, "they used to go down

---

7. Stephanie Redd Large, LaRae Harris Wilson, and Sarah Gonzales. Personal correspondence. 28 June 2022.

8. LaRae Harris Wilson, ibid.

9. Louise Hilton Jeter. Personal correspondence. 28 June 2022.

10. Jamie Erekson. Personal correspondence. 28 June 2022. And Taylore Wintch. Personal correspondence. 15 June 2022.

to the beach for long prayer meetings called 'wrestlings,'" so-named after Enos.[11] A common thread through these modern deployments of the Book of Enos is how readers sought to inhabit Enos's position. The modeled his praying. They repeated the moves of Enos's story in an attempt to make it their story too. In the example from Ghana they developed a ritual practice from Enos's experience and named it from his record. Modern readers of the Book of Mormon have approached the Book of Enos as an Every-body text, finding it relatable and replicable. They have tried to be like Enos.

The Book of Enos signals itself as a repeatedly enacted prayer, wrestle, and covenant, as an Every-body text. And as an Every-body text, the Book of Enos indicates that it is, itself, just one enactment in a series. At the end of Enos's prayer sequence, the Lord tells him, "Thy fathers have also required of me this thing; and it shall be done unto them according to their faith; for their faith was like unto thine" (18). This is not the first time for this prayer, covenant, or even this flavor of faith. Enos as an Every-body narrative is a tale of *the* iterative Lehite conversion and covenant. It begins and ends thinking of the words that have been heard by the fathers. Each time the story is told, the next generations can enact it as well.

---

11. James Goldberg, former church historian. Personal correspondence. 28 June 2022.

Eden, Enos, and Re-Creation

Rebekah Call

THE WORDS *Adam* and *Enos* are curiously connected in Hebrew: *Adam* means "human," and Enos similarly means "mortal" or "human." Could there be a parallel reading between the Garden of Eden account and the Enos account in the Book of Mormon? This paper proposes that the Enos narrative can be read as a recapitulation—a restatement, with variation—of the Eden experience. In this exploration, I will first illustrate the connection between Enos and Eden by briefly outlining some of the parallels between the two accounts, before embarking on a more in-depth analysis of other elements, including awareness, work, rest, and how the Enos account points to Christ as the ultimate goal.

1. Enos and Narrative

The story of the creation and the Garden of Eden is a fundamental part of scripture: it casts a long shadow over the Old Testament—if for no other reason than by placement! It serves as an origin story that creates the cosmic canopy under which the people of the Old Testament relate to their God. In Latter-day Saint scripture, the influence of the creation story remains a key part of the overarching scriptural cosmos, even as it morphs to become a vital part of the reasoning behind the need for Christ. Furthermore, the Garden of Eden is sometimes viewed as both the source and end goal of humankind. For Jews, the conception of the

11

afterlife can include a return to Eden: the Talmud refers to "the world to come," or "heaven," as *gan Eden*, literally "the Garden of Eden."[1] In some sense, this is similar for Latter-day Saint devotees, for whom Eden may continue to function as a goal, as saints around the world symbolically return to Eden as part of temple ritual.

Much as the creation and Eden stories of Genesis create the overarching framework of the rest of scripture, Enos also encapsulates what might be called the "Book of Mormon project." It is a story of an individual's journey to Christ, but it also includes reference to the other main narrative elements of the Book of Mormon as a whole: the Nephite and Lamanite conflict, the eventual destruction of the Nephite people, and the preservation of records in the face of that destruction. In a sense, Enos is the Book of Mormon in miniature. Moreover, if Enos is functioning as an Edenic narrative, then the Small Plates of Nephi (from 1 Nephi through Omni) creates a mirrored, or chiastic[2] response to Genesis and Exodus: Genesis-Exodus begins with creation, tells how God established a covenant that made a people chosen and gave them a land, and ends with the exodus of that chosen people (the Israelites) toward a promised land (the Holy Land). However, the Small Plates reverses the order: they begin with the exodus of chosen people (the Lehites) toward a promised land (the Americas) with a covenant binding the land and the people, and, if this reading is correct, it ends

---

1. See, for example, Ta'anit 31a:9; Berakhot 16b:18; Sefer HaIkkarim, Maamar 2, 30:8.

2. Chiasmus occurs frequently throughout the Old Testament as well as throughout the Book of Mormon. It is characterized by the repetition of thematic elements in reverse order (A B C, C B A). An example of this is found in Psalms 3:7–8:

A   Save me
  B   O my God,
    C   For you have smitten
      D   All my enemies
        E   On the cheekbone.
        E   The teeth
      D   Of the wicked
    C   You have broken.
  B   To Jehovah
A   The salvation.

with the re-creation narrative of Enos as a recapitulation of the Eden story. In addition, both of these accounts serve to frame their broader narratives, while functioning as their own smaller narrative units.[3]

I will now briefly describe some details that link Enos to the creation account in Genesis.

2. Names

First, I would like to dive deeper into the names of Adam and Enos. When reading Enos as a creation recapitulation, Enos can be read as becoming the new Adam. In Hebrew, *adam* means 'human.' Thus, when God creates *adam*, then God creates "the human." In fact, it could be argued that *adam* never occurs in the creation account as a proper name, but can be literally translated as "the *adam*," or "the human." The Hebrew word *adam* occurs 26 times in the creation account (Genesis 1–3). Out of those occurrences, only two appear definitively without the definite article, "the." In these two exceptions, it is clear that it is referring to humankind,[4] or to an unspecified human being.[5] Thus, "*adam*" stands to represent humankind.[6] Similarly, "*enos*" in Hebrew can also mean "mortal, human, person, man." While it does not occur with the same frequency as *adam*, it shares a similar semantic range. Thus, in this story Enos could be seen as the new Adam.

---

3. The Enos story, along with the small plates of Nephi, can be viewed as a larger chiasmus when paired with the Genesis/Exodus narrative. It should be noted, however, that finer points of the Enos narrative may not necessarily form a chiasmus with the finer details of the Eden narrative.

4. See Genesis 1:26–27. "Let us make *humankind* in our image . . . and let *them* have dominion . . . so God created the human . . . male and female" (emphasis added).

5. See Genesis 2:5. "The Lord God had not caused it to rain upon the earth, and there was not *a human* to work the ground" (emphasis added).

6. There are three occurrences that could be vague. See Genesis 2:20; 3:17; 3:21. Each of these refer to the human and the woman as separate beings, and in each case, the vocalization is *l'adam*, "to *adam*." There is a marked similarity between in the pronunciation of "to *adam*" (*l'adam*) and "to the *adam*" (*la-adam*). As the vowels of the text were passed down orally, and were not solidified in written form until ca. 1000 CE, there is a possible argument that these three occurrences could be read as "to the *adam*" (*la-adam*).

3. "I Went to Hunt Beasts in the Forest" (Enos 1:3)

Forests are mentioned rarely in the Book of Mormon. Outside of quotations from Isaiah[7] and Micah,[8] forests are only mentioned six times in the Book of Mormon, all referencing wooded areas in the Land of Nephi.[9] Thus, we have a double parallel here: Enos is in an area with many trees, which is how Eden is described. Both locations are portrayed as areas of plenty from which their inhabitants are driven out: Adam and Eve leave the garden after partaking of the fruit,[10] and the Nephites flee the Land of Nephi after ongoing warfare with the Lamanites.[11]

4. "My Maker" (Enos 1:4)

This appellation of God as maker, or creator, also suggests a link to the creation and Genesis account. In Genesis 1–3, God functions in the creative role as the maker of the earth and of all life upon it. In Enos, the usage of the term "maker" is perhaps notable due to its rarity: "maker" occurs only six times in the Book of Mormon.[12] Contrast this with "redeemer," which occurs over 40 times in the Book of Mormon, "messiah," which occurs 33 times, or even "savior," which occurs 12 times in the Book of Mormon.

5. "All the Day Long Did I Cry unto Him, Yea, And When the Night Came, I Did Still Raise My Voice High" (Enos 1:4)

In the Genesis account, each creative period is clearly demarcated using the following formula: "and the evening and the morning were the first

---

7. See 2 Nephi 19:18; 20:18, 19, 34; 27:28.

8. See 3 Nephi 20:16; 21:12.

9. See 1 Nephi 18:25; Mosiah 8:21; 18:30; 20:8; Ether 10:19.

10. See Genesis 3:24.

11. See Omni 1:12–14.

12. See also 2 Nephi 8:13; 9:40; Jacob 2:6; Helaman 1:11; 3 Nephi 22:5.

day [or second day, third day, etc.]."[13] Thus, this sentence in Enos can be read as parallel to the days of creation, with the reference to day and night. If this is the case, then Enos's wrestle may be seen as his own engagement in a process of creation. Alternately, this could be the day of Enos's *re-creation*, in which he hopes to become a new creature, or as Saint Paul would put it, a "new man."[14]

6. "My Soul Hungered" (Enos 1:4)

It is interesting that Enos refers to hunger, or appetite, particularly given the emphasis on eating (and the desire to eat) in the Eden account. Of particular note is the parallel to Genesis 3:6: "And the woman saw that the tree was good for food, and that it was delightful to the eyes, and a tree desirable for wisdom. And she took from its fruit and she ate." The hungering soul of Enos could also be a reference to the Edenic (and ongoing) human desire for knowledge, and perhaps the resultant difficulties: while learning through experience brings the desired knowledge, it also invariably brings mistakes and regret, highlighting the continuing need for atonement and redemption.

7. Awareness and Unawareness

At each step of the Eden journey, the humans become increasingly self-aware[15] until they finally realize their own nakedness, at which point God can cover them. This act of covering implies atonement: in

---

13. See Genesis 1:5, 8, 13, 19, 23, 31.

14. See Ephesians 4:24.

15. In the Garden of Eden, it does not appear that the human, upon receiving the breath of life and becoming a living soul, has self-awareness, since much of what follows is an exercise in the development of awareness:

The first human is unaware of being alone, but becomes aware of this through naming the animals. (There may be a literary connection between the human's naming of the beasts in Eden, and Enos's hunting the beasts.) Then, only after a sense of awareness dawns—both of self and (lack of) other—God separates the human into two beings.

The humans are not initially aware that they are naked, or that they have the potential for cunning.

Hebrew, the word "to cover," *caphar,* is also the word "to atone." *Caphar* itself does not occur in the Genesis account, however, there is a strong implication that the humans are covered when God kills an animal (possibly a lamb) and clothes them in its skin.[16] Thus, the Eden account *ends* with awareness of the need for atonement. In contrast, the Enos account *begins* with awareness of the need for atonement, as demonstrated when Enos declares, "My soul hungered . . . and I cried . . . in mighty supplication for mine own soul."[17] This focus on *supplication for [his] soul* presupposes that Enos is already aware of his own unatoned state. Presumably, this is because of the words of his father that sank into his heart, creating that awareness. There is a possible (maybe antithetical) parallel here to the words of the serpent that bring awareness to the woman. (Pointing out the potential of parallel is not meant as a judgment of Enos's father or the serpent. It is merely an observation.)

8. Concealment

While he is aware of his own nakedness/unatonedness, Enos does not seem to be hiding that fact from God. This contrasts with the man and woman in the garden, who attempt to conceal themselves and their nakedness upon hearing the voice of God in the garden.[18] However, Enos is making his location known: he is "crying out" for his own soul, possibly even shouting: the account notes that he lifts his voice so high that it reaches the heavens.[19] Then as in the Garden of Eden, there is a voice: "There came a voice unto me, saying, Enos, thy sins are forgiven

---

They seem not to be aware of conflicting commandments from God: to eat the fruit from every tree, and to not eat from the tree of knowledge. (The Hebrew grammatical form emphasizes: "you *will surely* eat from every tree!")

They are not fully aware of the consequences of partaking of the tree of knowledge. This becomes very important when the serpent enters the scene, which will be discussed later in this paper.

16. See Genesis 3:21.
17. Enos 1:4.
18. See Genesis 3:8–10.
19. See Enos 1:4.

thee, and thou shalt be blessed."[20] Since Enos seems to have already laid himself bare, God does not need to call him out from hiding. Rather, he cuts straight to the atoning/covering of Enos.

9. Trust

"And I, Enos, knew that God could not lie; wherefore, my guilt was swept away."[21] Why is Enos's certainty in God's truthfulness the reason that his guilt is swept away? It is possible that this also resonates with the Eden account. When the serpent initially approaches Eve, it does not offer her the fruit of the Tree of Knowledge. Rather, it plants seeds leading to doubt in God's word. Its question begins with the Hebrew particle *af*, which is often used to emphasize and enhance the intent of the subsequent phrase, thereby possibly emphasizing the interrogative, "Did Elohim *really* say that you could not eat from each tree?"[22] After the woman explains her understanding of Elohim's commandment, the serpent further elicits suspicion towards God's word: "you will not inevitably die, for Elohim knows that . . . your eyes will be opened and you will be like Elohim."[23] In this statement, the serpent implies that Elohim has withheld information and is therefore not to be trusted. When read this way, the serpent's deception has at least as much to do with Eve's perception of Elohim's trustworthiness as it does with the fruit. It is therefore possible to read the Genesis text as indicating that partaking of the fruit came as a result of Eve's beguilement into mistrusting God. If this is the case, then the inception of the Fall was not at the moment the woman ate the fruit. Rather, it was when humans first mistrusted God. The Enos account reverses that primordial mistrust in deity, with Enos's statement that he "knew that God could not lie."

At this point, it seems that the Enos account might actually reverse the narrative of the Fall. Enos does not mistrust God, and because of this, his sins are forgiven. Maybe he doesn't symbolically eat the fruit!

---

20. Enos 1:5.
21. Enos 1:6.
22. Genesis 3:1.
23. Genesis 3:4–5.

Accordingly, one might expect the story to be finished, to be wrapped nicely with a bow, since Enos has passed the primordial test of trust. The chiasmus is complete: he returns to Eden and to cosmic simplicity. Right?

Here is where we have a surprise. Rather than resolving, the narrative lunges forward into more strugglings and more diligent prayer, and then finally into the work of everyday life: preaching to the Nephites, warfare with the Lamanites.[24] These latter two mirror the *end* of the Edenic account, *after* the Fall: after Adam partakes of the fruit, God informs him that he will only survive by the sweat of his face and that he will have to work very hard before the ground will produce for him.[25] Work drives the account forward, both in Genesis and in Enos, and our understanding of *work* can help us understand *rest*.

10. Work

In the Eden account, there are two types of work described. The first is *avodah*, from the root *avad* (referring to Adam's work), and the second is *malachah* (referring to God's workmanship). *Avodah* has a basic meaning of tilling the ground, serving someone, or accomplishing something. This is the word used when God positions Adam to work, or take care of, the Garden of Eden.[26] The nominal form of this root, when applied to people (as opposed to activity), usually means servant or slave. There can sometimes be a meniality, or a sense of lower class that is implied in the usage of this root.

The second type of work referenced in the Eden account is *malachah*. The text informs us that the humans were created on the sixth day, and on the sabbath, God "completed his work . . . and rested from his work. And God blessed the seventh day and made it holy because in it he rested from all his work."[27] The word for God's work (*malachah*) in

---

24. See Enos 1:19–24, 26.
25. See Genesis 3:17–19.
26. See Genesis 2:5, 15.
27. Genesis 2:2–3.

this context has to do with handiwork or craftsmanship,[28] in contrast to the word referring to Adam's work (*avodah*). *Malachah* often implies a sense of excellence, or refinement.

In the Enos account, it is possible that both types of work are represented. Enos's account may begin with him doing something more like *avodah*—hunting—something Enos himself later associates negatively with Lamanite behavior.[29] This could align well with the meniality of *avodah* in Genesis. However, his 'wrestling' and 'struggling' may quickly transition to *malachah*—something more refined, perhaps, in his mind and in his soul. It is possible that this idea of craftsmanship may apply to Enos as he attempts, in his own day of creation, to re-create himself, and his many strugglings may be because he was not a very skilled craftsman in this regard. This is possibly evidenced by his question, "how is it done?",[30] and by his very convoluted process in communicating what he actually desires in his prayers regarding the Lamanites and the future state of Lehite records.[31]

11. Rest

Another element that may support this reading has to do with how Enos talks about rest. The Hebrew word, shabbat (often transliterated as Sabbath), means rest or cessation. Shabbat (sabbath) also plays a key part in the creation narrative, with God blessing the *shabbat,* because he ceased, or rested from labor.[32] Jewish scholars have debated whether the first *shabbat* after creation actually happened. Did Adam and Eve partake of the fruit sometime the following "week," and now we, as humankind, are awaiting the second great *shabbat*? Or perhaps the *shabbat* mentioned in Genesis 2:2–3 is a promised *shabbat*, and we are

---

28. The word *malachah* comes from the root *l'ach*, which has to do with sending. Thus, *malach* can refer to messengers (often translated as 'angels' if sent from God), or can refer to trade missions/business journeys, or handiwork and craftsmanship, possibly because handiwork is something one sends the hand forth to do.

29. See Enos 1:3, 20.

30. Enos 1:7.

31. See Enos 1:13–15.

32. See Genesis 2:2–3.

all still functioning on the sixth day of creation (the day of the humans, so to speak), after which God will bring peace to the world by bringing the great *shabbat,* when all creation will rest.[33]

Once Enos receives the covenant for the future preservation of records, he writes, "my soul did rest."[34] At first glance, this does seem to indicate a true rest. However, upon closer inspection, we find an interesting fragmentation of Enos's self: part of Enos (his soul) is acting as the agent, but not Enos himself. He writes that his *soul* rests, but not that *he* rests. Why this fragmentation? Maybe this implies that he has ceased from his *malachah*—the creative work of his mind or soul, and he thus rests mentally (soulfully?) but not physically. He no longer engages in the elevated labor of *malachah,* but goes back to the mundane and the menial everyday grind of *avodah.*

If we accept this reading, then because Enos still lives in a fallen world, in which a condition is that humans only eat "by the sweat of their brows,"[35] it is not possible for him, in an unfragmented state, to fully rest. That can only happen at his death, when he leaves the mortal, fallen plane of existence, as described in verse 27: "I soon go to the place of *my rest,* which is with my Redeemer, for I know that in him *I shall rest.*" Note the absence of any fragmentation. Enos indicates that *he,* not just his *soul,* will rest, implying a unification within himself.

Also of significance is the fact that when Enos refers to the *place* of his rest, it is not actually a physical location; rather, it is a person. He writes that the place of his rest is *with [his] Redeemer,* seemingly with a strong emphasis on *place.* But then Enos clarifies his statement, giving

---

33. A third option (although less relevant here) is that God rested; then that rest was shattered by the Fall, and humankind continue to profane the day of *shabbat.* (In other words, we are still living now in the first *shabbat* that God created.) In this case, we as creation are awaiting a redemption of the profaned sacred.

Enos's view does not appear to harmonize as well with this option, since he does not seem to hover on the sense of shattered sacrality. He does acknowledge the Nephites' iniquities as wrong; but true faith, or living in relation with God seems to be available *now* for anyone who desires it. However, true rest does *not* seem immediately available, at least based on Enos's writings.

34. Enos 1:17.

35. Genesis 3:19.

us one of the few unfragmented declarations of the text: "in him I shall rest." Thus the Redeemer Himself becomes the place of full Shabbat, or cessation, since Enos indicates that he will rest *in* him, not *by* him, or even *through* him. In this way, Enos recenters his aim: there is no looking back to Eden, just looking forward to the end goal: Christ. And this goal is more than being *with* Christ. It is *abiding in* Christ, just as Christ abides in the Father.[36] The full realization of this only occurs after death, when the self is no longer held bound by the terms of a mortal world.

In this view of rest, there is no full reversal of the Eden account in Enos. The chiasmus is never entirely completed. Yes, Enos has an edenic experience, but then his narrative drives forward through a fallen world that faces fallen trials, rather than ending in cosmic simplicity. In this sense, Enos parallels (rather than contrasts) the Eden account. However, the Enos account makes a major departure from Eden account in its conclusion: Adam leaves the garden and the presence of God to work, with no apparent (or explicitly stated) rest in sight.[37] But Enos struggles, works, converses with God, and looks forward to a final and complete rest in Christ. By making Christ the end point of the narrative, Enos brings his account full circle: he begins with his Maker, journeys through conversing with his Lord, and ends with his Redeemer. Thus, Christ serves as the source, the means, and the end goal of Enos's journey. So what is the point of this comparison of the two accounts? My takeaway is that the Enos story is Eden reiterated, but with Christ playing an explicit role.

---

36. See John 15:1–17; see also chapter 17, particularly verses 1–3, 11, 20–26.

37. This conclusion is based solely on what is written in the Genesis account, not necessarily other Latter-day Saint interpretations of the Eden narrative.

Words Sunk Deep: Indwelling, Necessity, and Reconciliation in Enos

Adam S. Miller

1. Ignorance of Causes

WITH HIS SINS FORGIVEN and his guilt swept away, Enos asks a crucial question in Enos 1:7: "Lord, how is it done?"

Enos has observed the effect—he knows he's been forgiven—but he doesn't yet know the cause. How was he forgiven? And why?

In this way, Enos is like all of us. At birth, he passed through the veil that divides "now" from "before" and, thus, he passed through the veil that separates this world's branching effects from their root causes. Having passed through the veil, Enos suffers from the fact that, as Baruch Spinoza puts it in the appendix to Part 1 of his *Ethics*, "all men are born ignorant of the causes of things."[1]

The problem that results is threefold.

Ignorant of causes, Enos is ignorant of God, his first cause.

---

1. Baruch Spinoza, *Ethics, Treatise on the Emendation of the Intellect, and Selected Letters*, trans. Samuel Shirley (Cambridge: Hackett, 1992), 57.

Ignorant of causes, Enos is ignorant of his father, one of his nearest causes.

And crucially, ignorant of causes, Enos suffers from the fact that he's ignorant of how to consciously *be* a cause, of how to act and not just be acted upon.

Framed by these three problems, my thesis with respect to reading Enos 1 is the following: that the pivot point in Enos's story of redemption comes *after* he's been forgiven, when he first poses this decisive question: "Lord, how is it done?"

The turning point comes when Enos asks: Lord, what is the cause?

2. Indwelling Causes

For Enos, his story about God—and his discovery of causes—begins with his father.

To start, it's helpful to note that, unlike other books in the small plates, the Book of Enos floats free of its causal genealogy. Though Enos begins with his father (Enos 1:1), he never says who his father is. He never names Jacob. And unlike Jacob who precedes him or Jarom who follows him, Enos also never names his spiritual successor (cf. Jacob 7:27, Jarom 1:15). These genealogical dots aren't hard to infer, but Enos doesn't connect them. He doesn't link himself into the larger family tree.

Add to this lack of linkage the weird chronology spanning the lives of Jacob and Enos—there appears to be something like a hundred and twenty-four years between them—and it's likely that Enos was a small child when Jacob died.[2] If Enos hardly knew his father, this makes a common problem all the more acute: the problem that it's hard for children, even in the best of circumstances, to understand their fathers.

Of course, this ignorance doesn't mean that fathers don't leave a deep causal mark. Being ignorant of a cause doesn't stop it from functioning as a cause. It doesn't stop that cause from working on us and through us, from shaping us and persisting in us.

---

2. See Sharon Harris's discussion of this chronology in *Enos: A Brief Theological Introduction* (Provo: Maxwell Institute, 2020), 21.

In a very real sense, every effect is "indwelt" by the causes that preceded it, just as every son is indwelt by the causal stamp of his father.

And this, as we're told, is exactly where Enos finds himself: though his father is long dead, Enos can't get his father's voice out of his head. That voice is still inside him. It's still working on him, still pushing, still creating new effects. As an active cause, that voice still has a kind of life and agency all its own. "I went to hunt beasts in the forests," Enos says, and instead "the words which I had often heard my father speak concerning eternal life, and the joy of the saints, sunk deep into my heart" (Enos 1:3).

This characteristic of his father's sunk-words—that his father's voice has a life of its own in Enos's head—is for Enos a hint, a clue. This autonomous voice in his head is a symptom of the fact that Enos's head isn't simply his own. It's a symptom of the fact that Enos—regardless of his ignorance—is caused.

3. Wrestling with Causes

Enos describes what comes next as a wrestle. "I will tell you about the wrestle which I had before God, before I received a remission of my sins" (Enos 1:2).

The irony of this wrestle is that it happens only once Enos is alone. It happens in the presence of God, "before" God—but it's not exactly *with* God, at least not at first, at least not directly. As with the biblical Jacob's famous wrestle with an "angel"—a description that already presumes too much given the opacity of the text—the nature of Enos's opponent is ambiguous: like Jacob in Genesis 32, it's only once Enos is "left alone" in the wild that "there wrestled a man with him until the breaking of the day" (Genesis 32:24).

But how does one wrestle alone? With whom is Enos wrestling?

Enos is wrestling with himself—after a fashion. Or, he's wrestling with some part of himself, with some part of himself that isn't simply the same as himself. He's wrestling, I would suggest, with some force or cause that indwells him.

Again, as pivotal as this is for Enos, it's not unusual. If you want to discover what causes indwell you—and, thus, wrestle with yourself—few catalysts are as potent as solitude and silence. So, for Enos, it's no surprise that his father's voice becomes impossible to ignore only once he's alone in the forest. It's no surprise that he must first be alone to discover he's not actually alone, that his mind and body are effectively indwelt by the voices and lives that caused him.

This, I would argue, is the precondition for his forthcoming struggle: Enos can wrestle with himself before God because he's discovered he's not just himself. He's discovered that every effect is irreparably intertwined with its cause.

4. The Grammar of Causes

The structure of this wrestle is obliquely mirrored in the grammar of the book's opening verses.

In verse one, Enos's first move is to name himself—twice. His first move is duplicate himself, simultaneously positioning himself as both a first person cause and a third person effect: "Behold, it came to pass that I, Enos, knowing my father . . ." (Enos 1:1).

On the one hand, Enos is the "I," the subject of the sentence. And on the other hand he is also "Enos," the object of someone else's attention and address. He's both at once, doubled and divided. "It came to pass that I, Enos . . ."

What induces this grammatical doubling of Enos into both cause and effect? In this sentence, the proximate reason is the introduction of Enos's father. "I, Enos, knowing my father that he was a just man—for he taught me in his language, and also in the nurture and admonition of the Lord . . ." (Enos 1:1). Structurally, Enos's father sits at this fork that makes it possible for Enos to wrestle with himself.

Moreover, Enos's description of his father also mirrors this same doubling: "I, Enos, knowing my father that he was a just man . . ." (Enos 1:1). On one hand, Enos knows his father—*my* father, he says—as a person, in the first person. On the other hand, he interrupts this personal connection with the insertion of an awkward, third-person qualification: "*that* he was a just man."

And, perhaps most telling, the end result of this forked grammar is that the sentence introduced by I/Enos breaks off without ever introducing an active verb. The sentence that begins in verse one is grammatically incomplete. It's an incomplete sentence. And verse two, instead of addressing the problem, opts to just start from scratch. "I, Enos, knowing my father that he was a just man . . . And I will tell you of the wrestle which I had before God" (Enos 1:1, 2).

Hamstrung in this way between his status as a subject and his status as an object, Enos doesn't yet know how to be active. He doesn't know how it's done. He doesn't know how to *be* a cause.

5. Hungry for Causes

Suffering his ignorance, indwelt by his father's voice, divided and hamstrung, Enos begins to wrestle with himself. His soul begins to hunger. "And my soul hungered," he tells us, "and I kneeled down before my Maker, and I cried unto him in mighty prayer and supplication for mine own soul" (Enos 1:4).

Enos's soul is hungry. For what would a soul hunger? What would satisfy a soul? There may be a clue in the roughly poetic structure of verse 4, rendered as follows:

> (A) And *my soul hungered*
>> (B) And I kneeled down before my Maker
>> (B) And I cried unto him
> (A) In mighty prayer and supplication *for mine own soul*
>> (C) And all the day long did I cry unto him
>> (C) And when the night came I did still raise my voice

Enos's soul hungers, and so he kneels down, and he cries unto his Maker for . . . his own soul? Enos's soul is, apparently, hungry for itself. Enos's soul, in some way, lacks enough of itself. Enos's soul is apparently hungry for *more* soul.

Is "mighty prayer" simply the sound of a soul rumbling with hunger for more of itself? Is Enos's soul hungry for a "whole" soul (cf. Enos 1:8), rather than a partial or inadequate or incomplete soul? What would this mean? What would it mean for a soul to be whole rather than incomplete?

My thesis is that Enos's soul—knowing itself only as an effect—is hungry for knowledge of its causes. Enos puts it this way himself: his soul, he says, cried out for its first cause, for its "Maker" (Enos 1:4).

This kind of soul, a soul that is cut off from its causes—a soul that's ignorant of its God and Maker, that knows itself only as an effect, a soul that isn't whole—is a soul caught in the grip of sin. Hamstrung by ignorance, sinners experiences themselves (1) as cut off from their Maker, (2) as inadequate or incomplete, (3) as random and haphazard, (4) as a passive effect, and (5) as powerless to act.

In terms of emotions or affects, the soul's incomplete sense of itself—as rootless, inadequate, aimless, passive, and powerless—expresses itself acutely in the felt form of guilt. Guilt is what it *feels* like to be ignorant of one's causes. Guilt is what it feels like to be inadequate and incomplete. Guilt it what it feels like to not be whole. Guilt is what it feels like to need *more* soul.

In itself, this guilt—like all pain, like all passive suffering—is pointless. But, as a clue, this guilt may be helpful. As a clue, guilt may be a powerful symptom orienting Enos to his missing causes. Prompted by the persistence of his father's words, Enos takes his guilt as sign and, as a sign, his guilt is transfigured into hunger: "And my soul hungered; and I kneeled down before my Maker, I cried unto him in mighty prayer and supplication for mine own soul" (Enos 1:4).

6. Necessary Causes

In response to his hungry heart-cry, Enos reports that, "a voice came unto me, saying: Enos, thy sins are forgiven thee, and thou shalt be blessed" (Enos 1:5).

This is, of course, a vital moment—though, for my part, I think the more important moment comes next. What results for Enos from this conjunction of forgiveness and blessing?

What results is that he acquires a new idea and, specifically, he acquires a new idea about something necessary and essential. What results is that he learns something about how God—as cause—acts. "And I, Enos, knew that God could not lie; wherefore my guilt was swept away" (Enos 1:6).

This moment might be read in a number of ways. However, for my purposes, I don't want to read this as an idea about God that Enos *already* had in hand before he cried out. Rather, I want to read this as a *new* idea Enos that acquired as a result of what the voice told him. I want to read this as a privileged example of exactly the kind of adequate idea Enos's soul originally hungered for when he asked for more soul.

Why might this specific idea about God be an example of what Enos was praying for? What makes an adequate idea different from an inadequate idea?

Inadequate ideas are partial or incomplete because they are ignorant of causes. Adequate ideas, on the other hand, are whole or complete because they link effects back to their causes.

In addition, as I've already noted, inadequate ideas, because they're ignorant of causes, also *feel* a certain way. In the register of emotions or affects, inadequate ideas feel rootless, aimless, passive, and powerless. They feel contingent and haphazard and accidental. They feel like the shell of an idea, empty and meaningless. And this, of course, is exactly the constellation of emotions that converge in an experience of guilt.

How, though, do adequate ideas feel? In the register of emotions or affects, adequate ideas feel rooted, directed, active, and powerful. With the cause of an effect clearly in view, with the two halves of the puzzle reunited, adequate ideas, as adequate, feel *necessary*. In short, an adequate idea will present itself as a necessity.

What, then, does the presence of God—as cause, as Maker—feel like?

God's presence feel likes necessity. God's presence feels like the following conviction: that things are necessarily what they are *and* that now we must do what must be done. God's presence feels both like the full and unavoidable truth *and* a moral imperative to act in light of that truth.

And this is exactly the kind of idea given to Enos's mind, hungry as it is for necessity. What does Enos learn? "And I, Enos, knew that God *could not* lie" (Enos 1:6). Enos doesn't learn that God "didn't" or "wouldn't" lie. Enos learns that God *couldn't* lie. Enos learns something about God and this idea about God presents itself as a necessity.

Then, anchored in this divine necessity, Enos finds his guilt swept away. Aligned with his Maker, he no longer feels inadequate. Grounded in God as his cause, he no longer feels incomplete, rootless, aimless, passive, or powerless. The connection between cause and effect has been made and the lights have come on.

7. Faith as Cause

We're positioned now at the fulcrum of Enos's conversion.

Having connected with God as cause, having felt that cause as a necessity, and having had his feeling of guilt thus swept away, Enos asks: "Lord, how is it done?"

Again, I think this question is open to multiple readings. In light of my thesis, though, I would suggest that Enos is not asking God for an *explanation* of what just happened. Rather, I think he's asking for *instructions* about how to do it again, himself.

Lord, how is it done? Meaning, "how does one do this?"

Enos has experienced God as necessary cause—this is critical—but now he still needs to address that third fundamental problem: how does *he* stop living as an effect and start acting as a cause? How does he become an active agent in his own right?

The answer, as God explains it, is to have faith in Christ. "And I said: Lord, how is it done? And he said unto: Because of they faith in Christ" (Enos 1:8).

What, though, is faith?

Here, on my reading, Spinoza makes another helpful distinction when he outlines two different ways of achieving adequate knowledge of causes. As he argues in Part 2 of his *Ethics*, adequate knowledge of causes can be achieved: (1) via reason, or (2) via intuition.[3]

Achieving an adequate knowledge of causes via reason is hard work. It's adequation by works rather than faith. You must painstakingly work step by step through the causal chain, identifying all the links, until the necessity of those connections comes clearly into view.

---

3. Spinoza, *Ethics*, 90.

Once their causal necessity comes into view, then you have knowledge. You're no longer ignorant of those causes.

The trouble with reason, however, is that while all causal chains ultimately link back to God, these causal chains are also infinite and, so, you can never reach God this way. You can get a sense for local necessities, but you'll never secure a grasp of a global cause or necessity.

But adequate knowledge of causes via intuition has a different shape. Rather than painstakingly working your way back through the local causal chain by way of observations and inferences, you instead have an immediate intuition of God as *global* cause or necessity. In one revelatory leap, you essentially skip the intermediate chain to intuit—especially in the form of an *affective* grasp of necessity—God as global cause. This intuitive grasp of necessity is, I think, something like adequation by faith rather than works.

In this latter case, you still get all the redemptive effects of adequate knowledge—for example, the dissolution of guilt and your empowerment as an agent—but without actually knowing the details of all the intermediate steps that compose the causal network.

Here, faith isn't a lack of knowledge or a blind hope. Rather, faith is a real, operational knowledge of God as cause—it's just that faith, unlike reason, doesn't claim to have adequate knowledge of all the *other* local causes beside God. To paraphrase Nephi, we might say: faith is a real intuition of causal necessity; nevertheless, faith doesn't know the meaning of everything that's necessary (cf. 1 Nephi 11:17).

Faith, in this sense, is a principle of power. It empowers us to act and not just be acted upon. While we can't understand or control all the causes that affect us—we'll always be indwelt and affected by all manner of voices and causes we can't control—we can grasp their necessity when we see them from God's perspective.

And this truth—perhaps counterintuitively—is redemptive.

First, it's liberating and empowering to stop wishing that things were otherwise and, instead, affirm them as necessarily being what they are. I am what I am. Things are what they are. It's liberating to see and affirm that this world truly is what it is. Truth, in itself, is liberating.

And, too, it's consequently liberating and empowering to then also feel in my bones, in light of these necessities, what must *now* be done.

It's liberating and empowering to be convicted about what I must now do as I submit to divine imperatives.

But as mortals the only way to do this—the only way to stop living as effects and start acting as causes—is to align ourselves, by way of faith, with *the* Cause. The only way to be active rather than passive is to act in God's name, as his agent, on behalf of what's necessary, placing our faith in Christ rather than our own ideas and desires.

8. Struggling with Causes

In Enos's account, this is exactly what follows: Enos, having faith in Christ, begins to act as an agent of his Maker, as an active cause now aligned with his ultimate Cause. And, tellingly, he does so by seeking the welfare of others. He does so by actively seeking the welfare of the voices and lives and causes that surround him and indwell him.

The difficulty of this work is that Enos, as God's agent, will have to commit himself to struggling in faith with necessities he cannot control.

What does this work—the work of faith—look like?

Enos starts by struggling as an agent of God on behalf of those voices and causes closest to him. "Now, it came to pass," Enos says, "that when I had heard these words I began to feel a desire for the welfare of my brethren, the Nephites, wherefore, I did pour out my whole soul unto God for them" (Enos 1:9). God, in response, makes Enos a promise: "I will visit thy brethren according to their diligence in keeping my commandments" (Enos 1:10).

This, though, is not enough and Enos, again, widens the scope of his concern. "And after I, Enos, had heard these words, my faith began to be unshaken in the Lord; and I prayed unto him with many long strugglings for my brethren, the Lamanites" (Enos 1:11). And God, again, responds: "The Lord said unto me: I will grant unto thee according to thy desires, because of thy faith" (Enos 1:12).

However, it's not until verse thirteen that Enos gives us a look at the specific form of "his many long strugglings" for his brethren. Anchored in faith, Enos must now go to work as an agent. But what does this work—on the ground, as an agent among a mass of other agents—look like? What form does this work take?

It takes, I think, the form of reason.

To his faith, Enos must add works. To his adequate knowledge by way of intuition, he must add adequate knowledge by way of reason.

Under the umbrella of faith in God, Enos's struggle with necessity takes the form of painstakingly working step by step back through the causal chain, identifying all the links, until the necessity of those connections comes clearly into view and those relationships are understood.

Here, this local work of producing adequate knowledge by way of reason takes the very specific form of a complex hypothetical statement that tries to map out the causal relationships at stake in his love for the Lamanites. It takes the form of those tangled, complex, local necessities that Enos unravels in verse thirteen:

> And now behold, this was the desire which I desired of him—that if it should so be, that my people, the Nephites, should fall into transgression, and by any means be destroyed, and the Lamanites should not be destroyed, that the Lord God would preserve a record of my people, the Nephites; even if it so be by the power of his holy arm, that it might be brought forth at some future day unto the Lamanites, that, perhaps, they might be brought unto salvation—

Or, if we abstract from the content of Enos's desire to focus just on its form, then Enos's reported struggle with necessity on behalf of the Lamanites would look something like this:

> If this and this, and also this happen, then God promises to do this, even if it also requires this, so that this might happen, and, perhaps, also this.

Here, Enos has the look of a man who's been struggling with a vast network of necessities beyond his control, a man struggling to reconcile himself with what he cannot change and still, "perhaps," leverage some of those implacable necessities to save some part of what he'd hoped to save.

The key, for Enos, is to engage with these local hypotheticals *only* under the sign of global (and categorical) necessities. His works must be a function of his faith in Christ. His work must unfold as an attempt to reconcile himself, in love, with all the voices and lives and causes he cannot control, working on behalf of their welfare without attempting to dictate the results of that work.

But Enos must be careful here. Because if his works stop being a function of his faith in Christ, then he'll end up back where he started. Whenever we attempt to dictate results, then we end up ignoring necessities and, once again, we end up rootless, aimless, passive, and powerless. We end up guilty all over again. We end up positioned as effects, cut loose of their causes.

9. Father as Cause

Enos's conversion, originally catalyzed by the indwelling voice of his father, is almost complete.

Operating now as an agent of the Lord, Enos is struggling—with all manner of complicated local necessities—on behalf of the Lamanites. But, despite the difficulty of this work, Enos won't let go. "I cried unto [God] continually, for he had said unto me: Whatsoever thing ye shall ask in faith, believing that ye shall receive in the name of Christ, ye shall receive it" (Enos 1:15). If Enos asks in faith, as an agent of Christ, for what is necessary, he is guaranteed to receive it.

The remarkable thing about this promise is its scope: it applies, God says, to "whatsoever thing" Enos asks in faith. Even more striking, however, is what Enos then decides to pray for.

Enos doesn't pray for "whatsoever" thing. Rather, with laser-like precision, Enos zeroes in on just *one* thing: "And I had faith, and I did cry unto God that he would preserve the records" (Enos 1:16). In response, God covenants with Enos to do just that: to "bring [the records] forth unto the Lamanites in his own due time" (Enos 1:16).

Enos is relieved. Having received this covenant, he finds the peace he's been looking for. He tells us: "And I, Enos, knew it would be according to the covenant which he had made; wherefore my soul did rest" (Enos 1:17).

This, it seems, is the happy ending we've been waiting for: wherefore Enos's soul did rest. But, from God's perspective, the story isn't over yet. Enos—though he doesn't seem to realize it—hasn't quite reached his destination. He hasn't quite come full circle.

To close the loop, God will have to proactively intervene.

For the first time, in verse eighteen, the voice of the Lord does not come into Enos's mind in response to a wrestle or struggle or pleading. For the first time in the narrative, God speaks without first being addressed. Rather, in verse eighteen, the voice causes *itself* to come into Enos's head.

God needs Enos to know one more thing.

God needs Enos to know one last thing about what Enos had, in faith, desired of God: "And the Lord said unto me: Thy fathers have also required of me this thing; and it shall be done unto them according to their faith; for their faith was like unto thine" (Enos 1:18). Here, God reveals to Enos that his desire is the *same* as his father's desire. "Thy fathers also required of me this thing," God says. "Their faith was like unto thine."

Enos's story *begins* when he can't stop hearing his father's words in his head (cf. Enos 1:1). And Enos's story *ends* when God reveals to Enos that Enos's own words—for a long time now, all through his many long strugglings, sunk deep in his heart, without his ever realizing it—*are* his father's words (cf. Enos 1:18).

This was the desire which Enos now desired: his father's desire (cf. Enos 1:13).

Enos, rather than suffering those words, had become their agent. What Enos had at first only heard, he'd finally learned to say.

Enos, as caused, had—in Christ—become a cause.

Inference in the Book of Enos

Michael Hansen

FAITH PLAYS A SIGNIFICANT ROLE in the Book of Enos. The book puts faith in relationships to words, knowledge, reasons, and actions. In this paper, I consider how faith is situated in the book by analyzing the way that it deploys the word 'wherefore'. 'Wherefore' appears six times in the book, and each appearance offers a way to consider the overall structure and lesson about faith. By cataloging these six appearances, and characterizing their roles, I will sketch a model for faith. My main observation will be that the 'wherefore's in the book can be understood as a certain kind of inference. In the book, these inferences typically begin with knowledge and result in action of one kind or another. I'll hazard a characterization of how these inferences might work according to a rule. They bear some similarity to what philosophers call practical reasoning, but they also have some striking differences from most of the going approaches. Finally, I'll comment briefly on the potential upshots about the nature of faith and prayer in the book. The model I arrive at will appreciate something about faith's relationship to knowledge, reasons, and action, while avoiding some excesses for each.[1]

---

1. There are many difficult questions about how a Latter-day Saint theology should go, and I currently have no considered view. This piece is an attempt to apply some rough academic tools to a reading of the Book of Enos.

I. 'Wherefore' Marks a Kind of Reasoning

The Book of Enos trades in the language of reasons. It contains six 'wherefore's, many 'for's, a couple of 'because's, a 'cause', and a very noteworthy 'how'— "Lord, how is it done?" (v. 7). These words invoke a large family of related concepts, which can be difficult to parse—they involve reasons, causes, and explanations. And in the book, we find this family of notions plus their relation to things like desires, knowledge, and faith. So of course, this topic is too big for this paper. There are stubborn philosophical questions in the spaces between reasons, explanations, causes, desires, and knowledge. My attempt here is to not saddle Enos with anything from specific philosophical traditions, and all the same difficulties with those positions will remain when I am done.

When the Book of Enos deploys a 'wherefore', it marks a kind of reasoning. The structure of that reasoning is what I am considering. Reasoning contrasts with the statement of a mere series. The book begins with a convenient example:

1. A Mere Series of Events

> "[A] I went to hunt beasts in the forest, and [B] I remembered the words which I had often heard my father speak . . . and [C] the words of my father sunk [sic] deep into my heart, and [D] my soul hungered, and [E] I kneeled down before my Maker, and [F] I cried unto him in mighty prayer" (vv. 3–4).

Notice that when Enos lists these events, they are merely conjoined with 'and's in the passage. The sequence—or maybe mere coincidence—is there in the text, but that's all. This format is not unusual for scriptural accounts. There may be substantive insights to gain in the relationship between the elements of the series. But notice that here there are no explicit explanations given, no causes named. There are simply 'and's.

Now, consider the difference that a 'wherefore' can make. Contrast the mere sequence of events from above with what follows:

2. The First 'Wherefore'

> "There came a voice unto me, saying: Enos thy sins are forgiven thee, and thou shalt be blessed. And I Enos knew that God could not lie; wherefore my guilt was swept away." (vv. 5–6).

This passage contains the first 'wherefore' of the book. It adds a kind of structure to its sequence, beyond the conjunctions and punctuation that we've already seen. 'Wherefore' marks a transition or inference of some kind, (e.g., 'therefore', 'for', 'because', 'so', 'thus', or other illatives). But there are different kinds of transitions. So my question is about the transitions happening in the 'wherefore's of the book.

Perhaps an old dictionary can help. 1828 Webster's shows how 'wherefore' can act as illative or interrogative, and it happens to give its own scriptural examples from the KJV:

> WHEREFORE, *adverb* [where and for]
> 1. For which reason. "Wherefore, by their fruits ye shall know them." Matthew 7:20.
> 2. Why; for what reason. "Wherefore didst thou doubt?" Matthew 14:31.

I think the first sense is much more likely than the second for the passage. Enos appears to be citing reasons in this passage, rather than asking a question with his wherefore.[2] Giving a reason brings with it another set of questions. For convenience, let's lay out the reasons for the conclusion in a numbered list:

(1) There came a voice unto me, saying, "Enos, thy sins are forgiven thee, and thou shalt be blessed."

---

2. Although, considering it as a question might be interesting: "Wherefore was my guilt swept away[?] And I saith: Lord how is it done?"

(2) I Enos knew that God could not lie.

(3) Wherefore, my guilt was swept away.

Where (1) and (2) are the reasons for (3), according to Enos.[3] Now, there is a question about how far back the 'wherefore' should reach. Here, I've taken the two immediately preceding conjuncts, but Enos might intend for his 'wherefore' to reach all the way back to everything that has come before, building up to the sweeping away of his guilt. Encounters with the divine must be so rich that it would be hard to capture them in a record, so it might be wise to mention as many salient things as possible in the account. Surely, there is some sense in which this moment depends on each of the prior events. But the answer to his prayer seems especially relevant, so I'm going to look at the nearby reasons. I think the transition from (1) and (2) to (3) must be theologically substantial. After all, Enos will soon ask, "How is it done?" (v. 7). And faith will play a critical role in that explanation. God answers, "Because of thy faith in Christ" (v. 8). But my interest now concerns the nature of the inference, not a full theology of guilt. So rather than look deeply at the contents of these reasons, I will focus on the overall form that this transition takes. That is, my question is about the nature of the inference more than about the content involved, insofar as they can be separated.

One way to take this transition is as a description of certain kind of causal explanation that involves a mere telling of goings on. For example, one might explain that a tree was swept away by mentioning facts about the rain and the soil becoming saturated, wherefore the tree was swept away. Such a 'wherefore' in the book would point to certain causes leading up to the event of Enos's guilt being swept away. His verbiage about his guilt being swept away might lean in this direction (including all the events of his life up to that point, or perhaps only the more immediate ones). Perhaps the power of the voice could have this effect on Enos when combined with his knowledge, as the power of the rains descend on the tree and the soil. If this is the model for

---

3. This instance resembles somewhat Aristotle's practical syllogism found in his *Nicomachean Ethics* and *De Motu Animalium*. It might also resemble a realization of an Aristotelian capacity to tie the knowledge to the particular actor in action. But I think there will be some differences as we consider the rest of the 'wherefore's.

the relationship, it would present the sweeping away of his guilt as an effect to be described.

However, I think that this reading of the inference in the book is less likely. It is always difficult to determine these points about actual inferences since the intent of the speaker/thinker is important to how the 'wherefore' is deployed. Given that the reasons cited here concern Enos's knowledge and their effects on his guilt—internal affairs of Enos's psychology—it seems more likely that they are to be caused by beliefs and the like than by other events.[4] Enos cites his knowledge about God, rather than a mere relation to God, and that he recognizes the voice, rather than that he was spoken to. This seems to me to cut strongly in favor of an inference that depends on capturing the reasons, as reasons, in the mind of the thinker, rather than just merely giving a description of happenings.

So perhaps it is in the making of the inference that Enos is rid of his guilt, a process in which Enos actively participates. In contrast to the causal description model where events can pile together to make an explanation of the event, on this view Enos needs to consider the content of the voice and judge its source, and use his knowledge about the voice, and *thereby* come to a conclusion that sweeps away his guilt. This would better capture the nature of Enos *making* an inference: after all, he cites his reasons. Rather than mere descriptions of something happening out there, we see judgements that connect together to produce a new judgement for the reasoner. So these details about testimony, knowledge, and guilt seem to press in this direction, with their inner lives, though I won't argue for that thesis here. Further, notice that although Enos doesn't immediately say who the voice belongs to when he hears it—he merely says that he hears a voice—the inference we find here won't happen without making a connection between the voice that appears in (1) and the God that appears in (2).[5] I think the

---

4. Guilt and the like are typically considered internal affairs. But for an account of shame that reaches further outward, see Lucy O'Brien, "Shameful Self-Consciousness," *European Journal of Philosophy*, 28/3 (October 2020): 545 - 566.

5. It is one thing to say that God can't lie, and another to say that God can't say false things, or must only say true things, or say all the true things. But the fact that Enos has God's inability to lie, rather than an inability to speak falsehood or the like, might show

contents involved in the reasoning, and the way that they connect, push in this direction for the form of the inference.

However, I will point out the strange form that the conclusion takes on this reading. Rather than concluding with a third judgment, or declaration of knowledge, or something else apiece with the nature of the premises, Enos's 'wherefore' leads to an event, or perhaps a process: his guilt is swept away. He doesn't say, "I, Enos, *believed* that I was forgiven (on the basis of the testimony from God)." Thus, the form of the conclusion is surprising. The form of the conclusion here leads us into interesting territory, and I think it signals an important element to the kind of 'wherefore' that Enos deploys.

In fact, as we have seen, his next thought is a question for the voice: "How is it done?" (v. 7). Now, there is a lot to ask how about when one encounters the divine—especially in hearing God's voice. The 'it' could be any number of things. Starting with the less mundane: how did my voice reach the heavens? How are you speaking to me? How are you so honest all the time? Continuing, and becoming ever more interesting: How are my sins forgiven? How will I be blessed? And finally, how is my guilt swept away? One way to read this move to Enos's question is to consider the surprise we had when Enos's judgements lead to an event. This kind of relationship between words and events is rare. Words typically attempt to describe the world, not to shape it. But these words brought Enos to this conclusion we see in (3).[6] He might ask, "Lord, how is my guilt swept away through this 'wherefore'?"

that Enos relies on the source of the voice, and his hearing of it, more than simply on the content that it brought. A plausible account of lies should include something about intent or communicative relation between speaker and hearer, such that the hearer is not intentionally deceived, or some similar formulation. If it were simply that the truth value of the propositions in (1) are established, and Enos is then left to himself to use them to arrive at his 'wherefore', then a reason about truth, rather than lies, would do the job. But we have a note about lies in the book, which seems to draw in the source in a more intimate way in the inference.

6. Here there is an opportunity to read "the words of my father." On one approach, Enos's father teaches Enos in his language. So on this reading, it might be that he taught Enos how to act on the basis of his reasons as they become articulated in language. Another take is to learn the divine language of God the Father, so that one can act on the basis of these reasons. Both seem to me plausible approaches to a language of faith.

In short, God answers, "because of thy faith in Christ" (v. 8). Here again, the nuts and bolts of faith (not seeing, etc), on top of guilt, offer plenty to consider for substantial theological positions. But again, I will focus merely on the 'wherefore' transitions we find in the book. How should we read Enos as making this inference, having faith in the above set of reasoning, such that it can sweep away his guilt? And we have a preliminary answer: because of his faith in Christ. Both question and answer will need further unpacking.

3. The Second 'Wherefore'

"Wherefore go to, thy faith hath made thee whole" (vv. 7–8).[7]

It is noteworthy that this 'wherefore' belongs to God, who gives it in response to Enos's question.[8] I can think of two ways this could go:

(1) Enos has faith in Christ and is made whole by his faith.
(2) Wherefore, Enos should go to.

Or else

(1) Enos has faith in Christ.
(2) Wherefore, God commands Enos to go to.

In the first case, the 'wherefore' issues as a normative reason. Since Enos has a certain quality, he should go to something. When one is

---

7. In Skousen's, *The Book of Mormon: The Earliest Text.* (United Kingdom: Yale University Press, 2009) we find a "go to it." The 'it' might encourage readings where something specific is in mind for the command to Enos, rather than a general "go to."

8. Whether God makes inferences is a difficult question. He certainly gives his revelations in the form of inferences to us. See Isaiah 1:18 "Come now, and let us reason together, saith the Lord . . ." and D&C 50:10–11 "And now come, saith the Lord, by the Spirit . . . let us reason together, that ye may understand; let us reason even as a man reasoneth one with another face to face." But what use could an inference be for God? "All things are present with [Him], for [He] knows them all" (Moses 1:6). To avoid this question, I will just treat the form of the text.

whole, it would seem reasonable that one should go to something for which one is now whole. If there is such a connection between wholeness and action, it would push in this direction. In the second case, we have a descriptive reason: Enos's faith itself opens up to God the chance to offer him a commandment. In this case, it seems like Enos is receiving the blessing of a command because of his faith. That is, thanks to his faith in Christ, God is able to command Enos to act.[9] In either case, Enos's faith plays a critical role in the inference.

4. The Third and Fourth 'Wherefore'

> "When I had heard these words, I began to feel a desire for the welfare of my brethren the Nephites. Wherefore I did pour out my whole soul unto God for them" (v. 9).

> "Wherefore I will visit thy brethren according as I have said" (v. 10).

Briefly, notice that these 'wherefore's both stand between words and actions, in one way or another. In the third 'wherefore', we find words, or at least the hearing of them, followed by a desire. That desire develops through the book, eventually becoming a conditional articulation about the future. And the desire eventually leads to the action of pouring out his soul.[10] In the fourth 'wherefore', we find a shorthand,

---

9. Further, by God's grace and Enos's faith, perhaps Enos is able to follow through with the commandment.

10. For well loved verses on the relationship between words, desires, and prayer, see Romans 10:17: "For faith cometh by hearing, and hearing by the word of god." And 3 Nephi 19:24: "It was given unto them what they should pray, and they were filled with desire." In my account for the desire in Enos, I emphasize the role of the words of the desire, and notice that the desire eventually arrives at some developed linguistic content.

The appearance of desire at this stage has some similarities to a Humean account of practical reason, where desire plays a key role in the action. Or more recently, similarities to a Davidsonian account of practical reason where beliefs and desires connect to actions. In Davidson's wake, discussions about this relationship tend to concern motions of the body. But notice that the resulting actions in the book don't seem so wrapped up with bodily movements. Enos certainly has some metaphorical bodily language, "according as I have said." This could simply be a reference back to the set of conditions that God lays out earlier. But I find it interesting that the shorthand refers to what is said, rather than to the conditions or terms themselves. Thus, among many moving parts here, I want to emphasize the relationship that holds between words and actions in both of these 'wherefore's. Moreover, the words in both cases relate to God. In the third appearance, the words cited are about Christ; in the fourth, they are from God.

5. The Fifth 'Wherefore'

> "Wherefore I knowing that the Lord God was able to preserve our records, I cried unto him continually" (v. 15).

First, note that knowledge appears as a reason for Enos's action of crying. The relationship between that knowledge and action is what's at issue. Different kinds of action can depend in important ways on the knowledge of their actor. One way this dependence can take shape is in the action taking a certain aim and object due to the knowledge of the agent.[11] Crying unto the lord *without* knowledge about His ability

---

but his cases seem to be unlike the paradigm voluntary moving of arms and feet. And rather than taking beliefs as inputs, the book cites knowledge about and words from God, instead. For these reasons, I think the inferences we have found in the book won't fit neatly into these accounts.

11. Consider the difference between running away from something, and fleeing in a generalized terror. Running from something requires you to be able to identify that thing in order to run from it. This mental layer of identifying introduces a problem for the action: the thing might not actually be there to identify in some cases. For example, consider a rabbit with an overactive danger registration system: the rabbit runs frequently from non-existent dangers. But these systems seem not to care whether they are right or wrong. They don't respect the truth as much as they respect expediency. In fact, an overactive danger registration system can add to the rabbit's fitness—after all, regular practice can improve the speed and reaction time of the runner, and spending energy on practicing in this way could be profitable for the rabbit, despite regularly being in error. For such a rabbit, it seems more likely that we find simple fleeing, not from any particular danger: anywhere is better than here!

However, the perceptual systems in rabbits work different than their danger registrations. Plausibly, perceptual systems aren't built to simply improve the fitness of the

to preserve the record, and crying to the lord *with* knowledge about his ability to preserve the record might even constitute different actions altogether. It is easy to see the difference by considering how things would go if Enos were crying to the Lord because of a lack of knowledge about God's power. In this case, his reasoning would issue in something different than his request, and more like a sincere question:

> (1) I Enos *didn't* know if God could preserve the records.
> (2) Wherefore, I cried unto God to ask him to try to preserve the records.

Or

> (2*) Wherefore, I cried unto God to ask him whether he could preserve the records.

Contrast the above inferences with the following:

> (1') I Enos, *knowing* that God could preserve the records.
> (2') Wherefore, I cried unto God to ask him to preserve the records.

The cry in (2), (2*), contrast with the cry in (2'). The difference is in the content of the cry, but also in the kind of act itself, due to the knowledge that the act depends on. Thus, the way that knowledge feeds into the 'wherefore' will change the kind of action that can result from it.

Now, if that's right, then the shape of the action that Enos is able to arrive at with his 'wherefore's from his knowledge fits the instructions that God gave him:

> "Whatsoever thing ye shall ask in faith – believing that ye shall receive – in the name of Christ, ye shall receive it" (v. 15).

---

creature, they function to discover the truth. And in this relationship to the truth, the rabbit would be able to do something more advanced. It would be able to flee from specific threats, and to sometimes do it correctly.

Thus, the 'wherefore' operates on the kind of knowledge that Enos cites in his reasoning for his action, and it empowers him to act in the right way. Enos's knowledge allows him to infer an action through his faith. As Enos puts it: "and I had faith and I did cry unto god" (v. 16).

6. The Sixth 'Wherefore'

> "I Enos knew that it would be according to the covenant which he had made; wherefore my soul did rest" (v. 17).

Here Enos marshals his knowledge in support of his concluding action:

(1) I Enos knew that it would be according to the covenant which he had made.
(2) Wherefore, my soul did rest.

Again, knowledge precedes the conclusion here.[12] But is the conclusion an action? Is resting an action? Why not? Consider the question, what are you doing? I am resting. That's a perfectly good response, and a perfectly good thing to be doing on the basis of your knowledge. In fact, resting with knowledge appears to be different than resting with ignorance. Ignorant resting, done without knowledge that things have been secured, is a mere diminishment of one's power of activity.[13] Running from tasks, ignoring reasons, and sitting down produces a kind of resting. Even the obedient dog that sits does so on the basis of some relationship to its owner (or treats). But resting on the basis of knowledge of God's power and its deployment in covenant offers a different

---

12. And here perhaps there is some resemblance to Kant's approach to practical reasoning. Is the inference pattern a kind of Kantian respect for a law that can account for an action? Or is the right model a kind of earlier rationalist perfection in knowledge such that one's reasoning proceeds from knowing the nature of some thing? Again, I think things won't fit easily into these approaches, but comparisons might still be profitable.

13. Even ignorant sitting may require a minimal knowledge—perhaps knowledge that the chair is comfortable, or simply knowing how to sit at all. Perhaps all genuine action requires some sort of very primitive knowledge. Typically, the greater the knowledge, the greater the power to act, though sometimes they come apart.

kind of resting altogether. The content of this knowledge allows one to rest with more security than the comfortable chair can offer, and instead one can expect the rest to last along with the covenant. This gives a certain kind of force and warrant to the reasoning that Enos appears to be engaging in. It is more than a guarantee of the truth of the conclusion, or powerful enough to issue in an action, though it must be both of those things. It warrants a certain kind of action that depends on the input knowledge, and an action in relationship to knowledge of God.

II. Reading Faith as a Rule for a Certain Kind of Inference

Taking stock of what we have seen, I think we can make some conclusions about the sense of 'wherefore' that is shared throughout Enos. Of course, it is possible that there are multiple senses here. In this paper, I capture something they seem to share, and need in order to make the transition as it is done in the book. I catalog these elements in the following table:

Wherefore	Input	Output
1st (v. 6)	I, Enos, knew that God could not lie.	My guilt was swept away.
2nd (v. 8)	Thy faith [in Christ] hath made thee whole.	Go to.
3rd (v. 9)	When I had heard these words [from God] I began to feel a desire for the welfare of my brethren.	I did pour out my whole soul unto God for them.
4th (v. 10)	According as I [God] have said.	I [God] will visit thy brethren.
5th (v. 15)	I knowing that the Lord God was able to preserve our records.	I cried unto him continually.
6th (v. 17)	I, Enos, knew that it would be according to the covenant which he [God] had made.	My soul did rest.

These 'wherefore's present a distinctive sort of transition in the book. The inputs share in being about deity, often as knowledge about God, or at least words from God (whom Enos has established as trustworthy in the first case). The outputs share in being a wide variety of action types (i.e., being swept, a command to act, a pouring, a visiting, a crying, and a resting). I have noted that faith accompanies each move, but not yet in what way. Faith doesn't appear as an element in either inputs or outputs, though its object, God, appears in each input in one form or other. Given these observations, the form of the 'wherefore' transition that we find in the Book of Enos appears to be captured roughly by the following schema:

(1) Some knowledge about God.
(2) Wherefore, a certain action.   (from 1, by the rule of faith)

So, if this is on the right track, I propose that faith plays the role of a rule for the inference for these 'wherefore's. That is, in the Book of Enos, faith is the rule that allows the transition from certain kinds of knowledge about God, to a certain kind of action.

III. Comments on This Reading of Faith

What I've sketched above is but one approach to faith in the book. What I can say for this model is that it accounts for some striking features of the inputs and outputs around 'wherefore' in the book. It also comes with some ramifications about the nature of faith. In section I, I claimed that these 'wherefore's can begin with knowledge, and can end with actions. In section II, I suggested that the role of faith between these elements can play the role of an inference rule. In this section, I will comment on what this sketch might mean for faith more generally.

This reading situates faith between knowledge and action. On this account, in order to make an inference by the rule of faith, one must begin with some knowledge about God (or at least some reliable words from above). Some accounts of faith instead seek to supplement a lack of knowledge, and criticisms of blindness closely follow. Not so for this account. It resists criticisms of blindness by incorporating knowledge as an essential piece of its input.[14]

By connecting the rule of faith to knowledge inputs, there is a risk of making faith a purely intellectual endeavor, never relating to any works.[15] Criticisms of dead faith are nearby.[16] But on this model, faith always issues in action as output. Furthermore, at the other extreme, this account also escapes the excesses of a purely pragmatic faith, because it incorporates reflection on one's knowledge of God as a key element. One can't simply go to work in faith without a relationship for whom one is working. One way to condense the model of faith as an inference rule is to emphasize how the model puts faith in a position of power: it treats faith as the power whereby the worlds were framed by the word of God, and the power whereby we act.[17]

On this account, faith can be had in various steps and degrees. Just as a child or a dog can reason without really knowing what they are doing, so can one have such faith without really knowing it. But just as a child can learn to recite a line of reasoning that fits a good rule, so can one advance in their faith—consider Enos's progress in learning how his guilt was swept away. And just as one can further understand a rule by stating it explicitly in language, so can one grow in their faith through learning how this piece of language works. And just as one can cite a rule whereby one acts, so can one invoke their faith in Christ in performing the action.

Finally, I think that this reading of the book turns Enos on his head. It is straightforward to read the book as a sermon about intense

---

14. Of course, this doesn't preclude this faith from increasing knowledge as it is used. As Enos explains "after I, Enos, had heard these words, my faith began to be unshaken in the Lord; and I prayed unto him" (v. 11).

15. Here, too, there is a concern that being faithful is more than performing a set of actions, but is instead akin to having a certain virtue of being faithful. Perhaps this virtue relates to the rule of faith, as having such a law be a part of oneself instead of a mere intellectual rule. I am indebted to my wife for this fine point.

16. See James 2:14.

17. For similar and familiar themes, consider what is found in *Lectures on Faith*. See Appendix 1: *First Theological Lecture on Faith*, circa January–May 1835," p. [1], *The Joseph Smith Papers*. https://www.josephsmithpapers.org/paper-summary/appendix-1-first-theological-lecture-on-faith-circa-january-may-1835/1.

desire in prayer. But on this model, the focus is not on the intensity of the desire, but rather on the content of the desire. The way that language, words, and records appear in the book is remarkable. Enos goes from words spurring his hunger, to words answering his questions, to words shaping knowledge and his desires, to using words in his actions. Rather than reading the book as a sermon on the role of intense desires in prayer, one could instead read the book as focusing on the words and knowledge of God in prayer, which can allow one to act by faith. We might call it learning a language of faith. On this reading, when Enos exclaims at the beginning of the book, "Blessed be the name of my God" (v. 1) due to his father, we can add further meaning to his father's language lessons: "Blessed be the *name* of my God," "for my father . . . taught me in *His* language" (v. 1, emphasis mine).

Elements of Salvation: The Pattern of Conversion in Enos and Other Book of Mormon Narratives

Elizabeth Brocious

1. *Ordo Salutis*

THE BOOK OF ENOS BEGINS with a story of personal conversion, one of many such narratives that the *Book of Mormon* presents. Across these various *Book of Mormon* conversion narratives, including the narrative in the book of Enos, certain elements are repeated such that they take on a pattern or formula in which a structure of conversion can be delineated. Such a patterned structure can be understood in terms of an ordering of salvific elements.

The idea of sequence of elements in the drama of salvation is found more broadly in Christian theology, specifically deriving from Reformed and Lutheran theology, designated by the Latin phrase *ordo salutis*, or order of salvation. In Reformed theological thought more specifically,[1] it is an understanding of how the Holy Spirit brings

---

1. In this essay, I focus on the Reformed history of the order of salvation rather than on the Lutheran because the context for the creation and publication of the *Book*

salvation to individuals through a chain of elements, which had been designated the "golden chain" early in the history of Reformed thought.[2] The phrase "golden chain" was first attributed to the series of elements listed in Romans 8:28–30:

> We know that all things work together for good for those who love God, who are called according to his purpose. For those whom he *foreknew* he also *predestined* to be conformed to the image of his Son, in order that he might be the firstborn within a large family. And those whom he *predestined* he also *called*, and those whom he *called* he also *justified*, and those whom he *justified* he also *glorified*.[3]

Paul's ordering, from foreknowledge to predestination to calling to justification and finally to glorification, serves as the basis upon which Christian theologians have engaged exegetically with this passage, for both systematic theological purposes but also for catechisms and sermons. More specifically, they have linked these passages to the eternal decree of God that designates some persons as being saved and some as being reprobate. Those who are saved are seen to be explicitly referenced in this passage as those who are first called and then as those

---

of Mormon seems to be specifically Reformed religious discourse as it developed in North America.

2. Richard Muller, "The 'Golden Chain' and the Causality of Salvation: Beginnings of the Reformed *Ordo Salutis* in *Calvin and the Reformed Tradition: On the Work of Christ and the Order of Salvation* (Grand Rapids, MI: Baker Academic, 2012), 161–201. See also J. Todd Billings, "Redemption Applied: Union with Christ" in *The Oxford Handbook of Reformed Theology*, eds. Michael Allen and Scott R. Swain (Oxford: Oxford University Press, 2020), 497–512. Both Muller and Billings make the observation that the elements of salvation that accompany the broader category of *ordo salutis* are generally understood by Reformed theologians as constituting various manifestations of the union with Christ rather than as temporal sequential steps that must follow a rigid order. Such an understanding of the elements allows for variances of interpretation of order and role that each element might take.

3. *Harper Collins Study Bible*, New Revised Standard Version, ed. Harold W. Attridge (San Francisco: HarperOne, 2006), 1921 (my emphasis).

who consequently receive the benefits of redemption through a forensic declaration of their righteousness (justification) and the final reward of a state of glorification with God.

It was not until later in the history of Reformed thought that the list of elements included in this chain was systematically expanded and formalized under the label of an *ordo salutis*, although the various elements above and beyond the original Romans 8 passage that found their way into various denominational and theologian-specific lists had been a part of Reformed theological discourse from the beginning.[4] Some of the additional elements that came to be variously incorporated into a systematized *ordo salutis* include regeneration, faith, repentance, adoption, sanctification, and perseverance, many of which were inferred either by the wording of Romans 8 (such as deriving adoption from the language of "large family" in verse 29), by terms that are present in other scripture passages, or by theological formulations surrounding justification and sanctification within Reformed theological discourse itself.

The order of the list can be seen to vary across individual theologians and even across Christian denominations, based on their own specific understandings of the doctrine of salvation, understood broadly. However, throughout all of the various thinkers who engaged in discussion of the "golden chain" or *ordo salutis*, whatever diversity obtained in terms of the specific lists of elements and their ordering, the one constant among them was the commitment to designating justification as the analytically separate act of God that bestows the actual gift of salvation. Such a commitment to retaining the specificity of a forensic declaration of righteousness represents an identifying marker of Reformed thought. This marker of Reformed thought shared this commitment with Lutherans as the theological hallmark of the

---

4. Truman designates the seventeenth century as the time period when the term *ordo salutis* and its accompanying systematized lists, which included an expansion of the original elements from Romans 8, came to take on its more formalized character in Continental European and English theological thought. See Carl R. Trueman, "*Ordo Salutis*" in *The Cambridge Dictionary of Christian Theology*, Ian A. McFarland, David A.S. Fergusson, Karen Kilby, Iain R. Torrance, eds. (Cambridge, UK: Cambridge University Press, 2011), 354.

Protestant doctrine that largely fueled the Reformation itself from its beginnings as well as what was responsible for the continuity of Protestant doctrinal identity as this theological movement spread across time and space. In other words, at the heart of the variety of salvific lists resides the constant commitment to a generally Protestant formulation of justification, declared by God, as the genuine moment of salvation. Any variations that include such elements as faith, regeneration, repentance, sanctification and so forth surround justification in varying ways but never replace justification as the moment of actual redemption.

The *Book of Mormon* does not participate in the activity of theological systematization that the *ordo salutis* represents. It is instead a series of narratives that depict religious experience. However, the book still presents a certain pattern in its conversion narratives that loosely follows the language and concepts that are found in the more formalized historical discussions surrounding the elements of salvation. It seems to assume not only a commitment to the framework of the standard Protestant salvific ordering through at least the conceptual presence of such elements as calling through preaching the word, repentance, and faith, but it also seems committed to a version of the doctrine of salvation in which a sinner who now believes is declared free of sin, and who once justified is subject to receive some version of regeneration or sanctification following this moment of forensic declaration. The *Book of Mormon*, thus, seems to be a case study in which the more technical or systematized aspects of Reformed theological discourse show up in popular religious understandings.

The fact that the elements of salvation that led to the systemized version of the *ordo salutis* were from the beginning a part of the devotionally directed, pastoral world of Christianity, such that they were incorporated into sermons and pedagogical methods of teaching (such as the catechism), suggests an avenue along which they likely traveled from elite theological texts to the pews. From these pastoral efforts, it may be surmised that at least the elements of the *ordo salutis* themselves, if not the specific Latin term, were distributed into and through the minds and hearts of those who lived out a Christian life. The *Book of Mormon* seems to be a record of the results of such a process of distribution.

For this paper, I compare various *Book of Mormon* conversion stories that exhibit some level of patterned articulation of the elements of salvation. My awareness of these patterns began with a close reading of the book of Enos, which itself exhibits a certain sequential ordering of the standard elements of salvation that are to be found in Reformed theology. From there, an analysis of other conversion narratives in the *Book of Mormon* yielded a comparative project in which the elements of salvation that make up the standard theological fare of the larger Reformed tradition do indeed show up in various ways consistently across the *Book of Mormon*. Thus, the book of Enos may be productively compared to other conversion narratives within the book itself, while they all as a group may be, I claim, interpreted in light of at least the salvific elements that are part of what has come to be called the *ordo salutis* discourse. This is not to say that all of the conversion narratives within the *Book of Mormon* are rigidly alike. They are not. But they do contain a similar general outline in terms of the sequence of salvific elements that show up in their stories. This paper seeks to abstract that general outline from the various data points we may observe in the narratives themselves.

The conversion narrative in Enos, however, contains at least one element that is unique when compared to the other narratives, and thus deserves some additional analytical attention. This difference has to do with a meta-theme found in the Book of Mormon itself: that of its own claimed status as a preserved record that passes on the preaching and conversion narratives of ancient peoples. Such a trope in Enos in which he is focused on the preservation of a record maps onto the role the *Book of Mormon* itself plays—indeed, as the very record Enos seeks to have preserved. This record is preserved precisely for the task of continuing on the work of salvation through a much broader time and space than what is depicted in the other conversion narratives in the book. This preservation of a record is foregrounded in Enos's story to the extent that Enos enacts a supplication for that record that parallels the supplication for his own soul. Thus, the preserved record is a major player in the drama of salvation found in Enos because it is seen as the mechanism through which the elements of salvation may be taken to remote believers across time and space.

2. The *Book of Mormon Conversion* Formula

The conversion narratives in the *Book of Mormon* do not strictly follow the order of salvific elements found in Romans 8:28–30, although we may sense a general implicit echo of the move to provide some kind of chain or pattern to conversion in the book. Indeed, the *Book of Mormon* presents at least three key elements, discussed below, throughout each conversion narrative, with additional elements appearing with enough consistency to suggest an assumed standard pattern to how conversion would (or should) generally proceed.

In addition to the Enos narrative, the conversion passages that I examine for this paper include the following: Nephi; the people of Benjamin; Alma₁ and his followers; Limhi and his people; Alma₂ and the sons of Mosiah; King Lamoni and his household, including his wife and servants, as well as his father, the king of the Lamanites.[5] In what follows in this section, I will present what I see as a broad formula of conversion based on these passages. Initially, I will leave out the conversion narrative of Enos in this analysis of the formula but will then use this formula as a framework in which to turn my attention exclusively to the book of Enos in the next section.

Preaching-Believe-Preaching

The most striking feature of my textual comparison of *Book of Mormon* conversion narratives is that preaching usually bookends the elements of conversion. Some explicit statement regarding belief is then wedged in between two acts of preaching. Thus, the most basic conversion formula is *preaching-believe-preaching*. Much of the structure of the conversion narratives from there constitute a kind of variation on a

---

5. See the respective references for this list of conversion narratives: Nephi: 1 Nephi 2:16–20; People of Benjamin: Mosiah 2:7–3:27, 4:1–5:15, 6:1–2; Alma1 and followers: Mosiah 11–18:1–18, Alma 5:1–13; Limhi and his people: Mosiah 21:28–36, 25:17–19; Alma2 and the Sons of Mosiah: Mosiah 27:8–24:4, Alma 36:5–24; King Lamoni and his household: Alma 18:40–19:36; Lamoni's father: Alma 20:8, 22:3–24:18. In addition, see Enos 1:2–23.

theme, such that preaching-believe-preaching forms a stable general framework within which we find variances in detail.

Preaching

The first instance of preaching in the *Book of Mormon* conversion formula is consonant with the idea of *calling* within the chain of salvation. Calling in general refers to the moment when a person becomes aware of a certain summons from God inviting one to faith in Jesus Christ. In Reformed theology, such a call is often spoken of as "external" when the source of the summons comes from the preached word, as opposed to an "inner" calling given personally by the Holy Spirit or the "effectual" call directed specifically to the elect, who then respond with faith and receive salvation.[6] The use of the word "preaching" in Reformed contexts most often assumes that the content of that preaching will be the gospel of Jesus Christ, inasmuch as preaching the "word" designates Jesus Christ as the Word (i.e., the incarnate form of God's word or utterance).

We see this assumption play out as well in the *Book of Mormon* conversion narratives as these narratives predominantly enact the concept of an external call through preaching. When other topics than Christ proper are preached, such as the ten commandments, history of the Fall of Adam, or prophesies, these topics are always subsumed under the larger pretext of converting souls through the promise of the redeeming acts of Jesus Christ. For example, King Benjamin and Abinadi both preach the law in the guise of the "commandments" of God but within the frame of the necessity of Jesus Christ to bring salvation.[7] Other preachers, such as Aaron in his speech to the Lamanite king, begin the narrative with the creation of the world and Adam's fall as a prelude to the work of Christ.[8] (Such preaching as Aaron's could perhaps be designated "teaching," especially since the term "teaching" is actually used in some of these passages where the idea of preaching

---

6. *The Westminster Dictionary of Theological Terms*, 2nd ed., Donald K. Kim, ed. (Louisville, KY: Westminster John Knox Press, 2014), pp. 53–54.

7. Mosiah 2:9–3:27, Mosiah 11–16.

8. Alma 22:12–14. Ammon teaches the same to king Lamoni (Alma 18:36–39).

would otherwise be present.)[9] Other preachers prophecy of the coming of Jesus Christ.[10]

Preaching the word as *calling* in the *Book of Mormon* most often comes from human beings such as fathers or prophets, as opposed to from God directly, although angels and/or God do make an appearance on two occasions. An angel delivered a message to king Benjamin, which he then delivered to his people.[11] But we see no conversion narrative for Benjamin specifically, only among the people he preaches to. The narrative of conversion here, then, depicts a preaching interaction between mortals (Benjamin and his people); the angel is merely the one who trains Benjamin in the content of that preaching. On another occasion, that of the conversion of Alma$_2$, an angel does indeed play a part in teaching the word of God unto conversion. In the initial telling of the story, the angel is depicted as saying words that are more of a rebuke and exhortation to Alma$_2$ than the preaching of the word,[12] although Alma$_2$ does then proceed to relate that the Lord was the one to tell him of the need to be born again.[13]

However, when Alma$_2$ later recounts the experience to his son Helaman, the structure of the story proceeds with the standard pattern in which Alma$_2$ remembers the words of his father concerning Jesus Christ's atonement, and it was these words that seem to be the catalyst for his moment of redemption.[14] Such is the case for Nephi also: even though it is God who softens his heart, his moment of belief follows from his memory of the words spoken by his father.[15] What's more, words that induce conversion are relayed orally. In all of the conversion stories, it is

---

9. Alma1 "teaches" and "preaches" to his people in Mosiah 18:7, and again "teaches" when king Limhi is present (Mosiah 25:17). When churches are established in the Lamanite kingdom, Aaron sends out priests and teachers to "preach and teach the word of God" (Alma 23:4).

10. As Alma2 remembers his father preaching (Alma 36:17) or as Lamoni's wife does as she awakens from her falling exercise (Alma 19:13).

11. Mosiah 4:1.

12. Mosiah 27:11–18.

13. Mosiah 27:25, although in his later retelling of the story, Alma2 states it was an angel who had "made these things known unto me" (Alma 36:5).

14. Alma 36:17–19.

15. 1 Nephi 2:16–20.

never the case that the written word acts as the sole catalyst for conversion, although written words do play a part in some of the narratives.[16]

Believe

In the *Book of Mormon*, the term "believe" is usually connected to the preaching of words, such that the one who is converted "believes" the words that are preached to be true. This belief is not just a mere intellectual assent regarding the correctness of concepts but a deeply experiential conviction that leads sometimes to fear, sometimes to joy, other times to dramatic episodes of unconsciousness, and, in the instance of Alma$_2$, to a beatific vision of God. But notwithstanding any supernatural elements that are present in a conversion narrative, the term "believe" is consistently linked, as noted above, to the preaching of human actors. For example, after Nephi cries to the Lord and the Lord softens his heart, he says that he "believed all the words which had been spoken by my father." Likewise, after he related his conversion to his brothers, Sam then "believed in my words."[17] Additionally, the people of Benjamin, after hearing the law preached by their king, cried out for the mercy of Christ's atoning blood because they "believe in

---

16. King Benjamin's words are relayed orally and in written form. However, they were written only because the crowd was so large that not everyone could hear him. For all intents and purposes, the sermon is an oral one (Mosiah 2:8–9). Alma1 writes the words of Abinadi (Mosiah 17:4), and we could possibly presume that that written record plays a part in his subsequent preaching and teaching, but again the interactions between him and his followers are depicted as predominantly oral interactions. King Limhi's relationship to written records is worth noting. First, Ammon preaches to Limhi and his people the words of king Benjamin, which were obviously derived from the written record Benjamin ordered to be made (Mosiah 7:3). But it seems to be Ammon's oral preaching that creates Limhi's desire to be baptized, which is later done by Alma1 after Alma1 himself orally teaches Limhi (Mosiah 25:17–18). Engravings also show up in the story of Limhi, who was "filled with joy" to learn king Benjamin had the ability to decipher them (Mosiah 21:28), but, again, Limhi's conversion doesn't seem to be linked to these engravings directly. Finally, Alma2 speaks to his son Helaman of the records that will be passed on to him, exhorting Helaman to keep them sacred. Once more, records of this kind play no role in the conversion narrative Helaman hears his father relate.

17. 1 Nephi 2:16–17.

Jesus Christ the Son of God." Later, when Benjamin asks them directly if they believe his words, they "all cried with one voice, saying, Yea, we believe all the words which thou hast spoken unto us."[18] Indeed, Alma₁ believed Abinadi, and Alma₁'s followers then believed him; King Lamoni, his wife, and those converted within his household all declare that they believe the words they heard preached; and later thousands of the Lamanites are converted because they believed. The premise in these conversion stories regarding preaching seems to be that the word of the preacher is equated to the word of God, and as such, carries with it enough force to bring about some change in a person. The "word" seems to be an agentive force that brings about such belief.

What can be referred to as the "salvific moment" takes place here in the step of belief. It is the moment, sometimes extended, in which various elements of salvation play out. It is the point in the formula in which the actual movement of conversion takes place, that is, when the various salvific elements combine to turn the believer toward God. The elements in the salvific moment that show up in any given narrative are not exactly the same across narratives, although there is enough repetition across the various narratives to manifest a general pattern. These elements are among the same that have played out through the history of Reformed theology in discussions of the ordering the salvific elements.

Such traditional elements of salvation that have an obvious role in the *Book of Mormon* narratives include repentance, faith, regeneration, and perseverance. Others that are less obvious but still show up are sanctification and adoption. Interestingly, justification, that centerpiece of Reformed soteriology, is often merely assumed in the *Book of Mormon* conversion narratives but still, I would argue, plays a significant role precisely as that which is assumed to warrant the entire sequence of elements.

Repentance. In its most general sense, repentance has been seen in Christian theology as the act of recognizing and expressing remorse for the presence of sin in one's life. It has often been linked to contrition and penitence. In Reformed theology, it was given a more technical place within the *ordo salutis* as a change of mind that involves the

---

18. Mosiah 4:2 and 5:1–2.

mortification (i.e., the "putting to death") of sin.[19] In the evangelical religion of the American revivals, repentance was often spoken about in terms of being "convicted" of one's sins through the Holy Spirit. This conviction then brought about the first stirrings of faith. In the *Book of Mormon* narratives, repentance is sometimes manifest through the act of crying out, often as prayers to God or as a response to the preaching either remembered or just heard.[20] It is also sometimes manifest through expressions of fear.[21] In the most extreme examples, the convicted sense they are surrounded by the yawning jaws of hell and fall to the ground as if dead.[22] For example, Alma$_2$, the entire household of king Lamoni, as well as Lamoni's father all fall to the ground and lose consciousness. Alma$_2$ speaks specifically of being "racked with eternal torment" and "harrowed up to the greatest degree" because of his sins.[23]

Faith. Faith, of course, occupies a central place in Protestant theology. Martin Luther was the first to construct faith anew as not merely an intellectual assent to the teachings of the church but an experiential movement within the soul that results in an abiding trust in God's promises. Reformed theology as a whole basically agreed with Luther's definition of faith, and the element of faith so understood continued to have a central place in the version of Reformed theology that took hold in America, including in its revivalistic embodiments on the frontier. In terms of faith's relationship to the other elements within the sequence of salvation, faith often hovers around the element of justification in Reformed theology, often acting as a precursor, along with repentance, to justification.[24] It is also spoken of as a cause to justification, although in its more scholastic renderings, Reformed theology spoke of this more as a logical, rather than an efficient, cause.[25] In the *Book of Mormon*, faith is also spoken about in causal language. The people of Benjamin have

---

19. *Cambridge Dictionary,* p. 443.

20. Examples are Nephi (1 Nephi 2:16), the people of Benjamin (Mosiah 4:2, 5:2), and the Lamanite king (Alma 22:17).

21. The people of Benjamin (Mosiah 4:1).

22. Alma2 (Mosiah 27:18–19).

23. Alma 36:12.

24. Muller, *Calvin and the Reformed Tradition,* p. 235.

25. Ibid, 240–1.

a remission of sins and peace of conscience because of their "exceeding faith."[26] Alma₂ tells us his father had a "mighty change wrought in his heart" because of his faith.[27] The queen who believed Ammon's words also is described as being blessed because of her "exceeding faith."[28]

Justification. In Reformed theology, the rendering of justification as a forensic declaration by God means to suggest that God declares a person righteous precisely through the righteousness of Jesus Christ, despite the fact that the actual unrighteousness of the person is not removed or taken away. It is a legal act with resonances of judgment.[29] This concept originates with Luther's doctrine of imputation, in which God reckons a person righteous as that person shares in the righteousness of Christ, which is offered as a free gift. As such, justification as an imputation of righteousness is distinct from the process of sanctification, in which the redeemed are made holy through the Holy Spirit working in them. Imputation of righteousness is declared based solely on faith or trust in God's promises. Theologians from the Reformed tradition maintained a basic Lutheran conception of forensic justification, agreeing with Luther that justification is the actual moment of salvation, which stands apart, at least analytically, from the other elements in the order of salvation. The effect of justification is that God's declaration removes actual guilt associated with sin as well as any penalties, and as such, peace of conscience is often associated with it.[30]

The concept of justification does make an appearance in the *Book of Mormon* conversion narratives, although surprisingly not always as explicitly as one might expect. The use of the term "justification" specifically is not to be found in these narratives; instead, the phrase "remission of sins" is sometimes used. The narrative that relates the conversion of the people of Benjamin depicts the most traditional version of Reformed justification. It relates that after the Spirit of the Lord came upon the people, they were "filled with joy, having received a remission of their sins and having peace of conscience because of the

---

26. Mosiah 4:3.
27. Alma 5:11.
28. Alma 18:10.
29. *Westminster Dictionary*, p. 192.
30. *Westminster* Dictionary, p. 281.

exceeding faith which they had in Jesus Christ."[31] The only other narrative that depicts an actual declaration that sins have been remitted is in Enos, whose narrative we will turn to in a moment.

Although other *Book of Mormon* conversion narratives do not use such language of remittance of sins as a way to relate the moment of a clear declaration of justification from God, I suggest that any narrative that invokes the idea of belief and faith within the context of preaching of the word and repentance, along with a resulting joy or peace, is assuming some version of justification as having taken place. In other words, the idea of a conversion narrative as such, told within the context of Protestantism, rests on the idea of justification as the concept that underwrites the whole religious experience being depicted.

However, a strictly forensic declaration of imputed righteousness may not be the version of justification assumed in the *Book of Mormon* narratives. In Alma$_2$'s conversion, we see him invoke the traditional elements of external calling and repentance along with an explicit statement that he has been "redeemed of the Lord." But the change he next refers to is not a mere imputation of righteousness but an actual change in state, a change from a "carnal and fallen *state* to a *state* of righteousness, being redeemed of God."[32] This language suggests Alma$_2$ is indeed *made* righteous, not merely reckoned as such. Such language indicates that, at least in Alma$_2$'s narrative, the elements of justification and regeneration, or even sanctification, broadly construed, are conflated into one moment.[33] While the type of justification found within the *Book of Mormon* deserves its own study, it is sufficient for us here to note that the general concept of justification is not just present in

---

31. Mosiah 4:3.

32. Mosiah 27:25, my emphasis.

33. Such a conflation would be considered a theological misstep in traditional Reformed theology inasmuch as sanctification was often understood to involve good works of some kind. But in Alma2's conversion, this sanctification is not the result of works on his part but is a free gift from God. It is an instance more of a miraculous regenerative change in the actual state of an individual rather than the traditional understanding of using means (i.e., works) to build a life toward sanctification—of course, with the understanding that these means have as their source and origin the power of God's grace.

these narratives, but it seems to be taken for granted as the central "hinge" moment where the believer turns from the repentant state to the regenerate state—this is, taken for granted that the term "faith" signifies its close cousin, justification.

Regeneration and Sanctification. A regenerate individual is one who has undergone some kind of transformation, a new birth, which enables a new life in Christ. Thus, the language of being "born again" signifies the concept of regeneration. Regeneration traditionally sets a newly converted individual on the lifelong path of becoming holy, i.e., on the path toward sanctification. The concept of sanctification can thus be understood as the broader rubric under which this initial spark of being made new is the initial starting point, and which arrives at its fullness when a Christian life is infused with a fullness of the Holy Spirit.

In the *Book of Mormon* narratives, regeneration is designated by phrases such as "a mighty change in us or in our hearts"[34] or Alma₂'s repeated use of the imagery of being "born of the Spirit" or being "born of God" to the extent of invoking the traditional element of adoption, i.e., "becoming [God's] sons and daughters."[35] The newly converted also experience great joy, sometimes to the point of overwhelming joy. For example, after his initial episode of falling to the ground in unconsciousness in order to experience his moment of justification, king Lamoni awakens briefly to declare his joy, only to sink down again, being "overpowered by the Spirit."[36] The queen also sinks down but arises later blessing Jesus and speaking in tongues as an expression of her profound joy.[37] Alma₂ relates that his soul was so filled with joy that he was able to see in vision God sitting upon his throne. As we noted with Alma₂'s narrative above, the effects of regeneration in these stories are both quick and profound, leading the converted to an almost instantaneous state of blessedness and holiness that might more traditionally be depicted as the result of a long life of sanctified living.

---

34. People of Benjamin, Mosiah 5:2. Similar language is used to describe the regeneration of the followers of Alma1 in Alma 5:13.

35. Mosiah 27:25, 28.

36. Alma 19:13.

37. Alma 19:29–30.

Conditional Perseverance. Perseverance is another traditional element in the *ordo salutis*, related to the journey toward sanctification as the converted continue to believe in God and to consequently live the type of life that secures their redeemed status. The *Book of Mormon* also invokes this idea of perseverance but often adds to it a conditional, something to the effect that *if* the converted keep God's commandments, only *then* will they be kept safe in their redeemed state.[38] Such is the message to Nephi.[39] Benjamin relates a similar message to his people when he tells them that only if they always remember the greatness of God and their own nothingness, as well as remain steadfast in their belief in God, will they then retain a remission of their sins.[40] Many of the narratives depict the newly converted as entering into covenant with God, and then marking that covenant through baptism and/or the formation of churches.[41] All of these acts constitute efforts to remain faithful to the end and to thus be preserved by God in their redeemed state.

---

38. *Conditional* perseverance, as opposed to just perseverance as such, is understood to be a feature of theology with Arminian leanings, such as Methodism. Christopher C. Jones draws a connection between Methodist conversion narratives and Joseph Smith's First Vision. I would argue that the *Book of Mormon* is another Smithian text in which we can trace such Methodist influence, particularly with its presence of conditional perseverance. The compilation of the *Book of Mormon* conversion narratives lands squarely in Smith's earlier years when Jones describes Smith as explicitly citing Methodism as an influence on him. See Jones, "The Power and Form of Godliness: Methodist Conversion Narratives and Joseph Smith's First Vision," *Journal of Mormon History* 37.2 (Spring 2011): 88–114.

39. 2 Nephi 2:20—as well the inverse promises of curses directed at Laman and Lemuel if they rebel.

40. Mosiah 4:11–12, 26–30.

41. Specifically, the people of Benjamin enter into covenant with God (Mosiah 5:5); the followers of Alma1, including king Limhi, are baptized and form a church (Mosiah 18:10, 16; 25:17–18); after the conversion of king Lamoni and his household, many more of his people are baptized and established a church (Alma 19:35); after Lamoni's father was converted, Aaron and his companions were free to establish churches in the Lamanite cities (Alma 23:4–5).

Preaching

Once the narratives move beyond the salvific moment designated by some kind of declaration of belief and its accompanying elements of repentance, justification, regeneration, and promise of perseverance, they move onto the next round of preaching, this time undertaken by those who have been newly converted. It is as if the most natural instinct that the newly converted experience after conversion is to turn to others and proclaim the message that brought about such profound change for themselves. Thus, the preaching-believe-preaching formula often has a cascading effect such that the now-converted preach to others, who then repeat generally the same conversion that the first preacher had already undergone.

For example, the conversion of Alma$_1$ occurs as a result of hearing Abinadi preach. Alma$_1$ believes Abinadi's words, repents, and then preaches to others. Those who then hear Alma's words in turn have a change of heart, with the result that Alma's words are transmuted in them into a trust in God. We see a similar pattern in the story of Ammon and the Lamanite people he converted. Ammon is converted presumably through the same processes as those that converted his companion Alma$_2$, and then he, along with is brothers, express a desire to convert the Lamanites. Ammon thus preached to the Lamanite king Lamoni and his wife the queen, whose dramatic conversions resulted in Lamoni then preaching to his people upon awakening. Many then believed Lamoni's words and were converted. The instances when the formula preaching-believe-preaching is not depicted as carrying all the way through to the second preaching and to a further line of conversions is when the narrative involves the conversion of a large body of people rather than single individuals, such as the people of Benjamin or the people of Alma.

Symbiosis of Public and Private. One common critique of the *ordo salutis* in Christian theology is that it places an inordinate emphasis upon the individual and thus overlooks any corporate aspects of salvation.[42] However, the idea that salvation occurs only within the context

---

42. Trueman, "*Ordo Salutis*," p. 355.

of a lone individual's private striving before God is one that does not generally hold as a pattern across the *Book of Mormon* narratives—although, notably, Enos is an exception. Rather, conversion narratives in the *Book of Mormon* generally depict a sort of symbiosis between the public and private, the internal and external. The preaching is usually performed publicly in the midst of groups or even crowds of people. Even in instances where a person remembers the words of a father, such as in the case of Alma$_2$, those preached words were originally delivered publicly. The moment of belief, then, is interwoven with the community each believer is connected to.

To be sure, much of the seminal salvific action does occur internally, such as the grappling of the reality of one's own sinful state or the softening of one's heart in repentance. But in some of these narratives, the body becomes a public sign for that internal drama. Such is the case when Alma$_2$ is struck dumb and unable to move and when king Lamoni, his wife, and his servants, as well as his father, all fall to the ground as if they were dead. Their body enters a holding pattern while the internal salvific work is accomplished, but their bodies become an outward sign for others precisely as such salvific action is carried out in a public setting. Once that individual salvific moment is passed, the newly converted commences the public work of preaching the word to others. In some cases, conversion leads to the ritual of baptism, another outward bodily sign of the inward status of being saved.

3. Enos's Conversion

With this conversion narrative framework in place, we are now ready to turn our attention to the book of Enos and to see how the conversion narrative there compares to the general *Book of Mormon* pattern. We will focus on verses two through twenty-three specifically. These verses illustrate the general pattern of preaching-believe-preaching detailed above but can be broken up in the following way. Verses two through eight depict Enos's own personal conversion in which we see him enact the first preaching and the salvific moment catalyzed by his belief.[43] Verses nine through eighteen serve as a sort of holding point in which the second round of preaching is delayed while Enos bargains with the Lord over the fate of his "brethren" the Nephites. Within these verses, Enos offers three prayers, one for his fellow Nephites, one for the Lamanites, and one for the preservation of records.[44] My analysis will focus on the first and third of these prayers. Verses nineteen through twenty-three then resume the pattern of a second preaching on the part of Enos, but with far different results than many of the other *Book of Mormon* conversions we just examined.

Personal Redemption

Enos's personal conversion follows the first two steps of the formula, that is, preaching-believe, and we can fill in the details of his conversion with the following *ordo salutis* elements: calling, repentance, faith, justification, and regeneration. He is externally *called* through the power of the words of his father, which, of course, constitutes the first instance of preaching. Such preaching leads to Enos's salvific moment of belief, which begins with his intense supplication that constitutes his *repentance*, enacted as crying to the Lord for his soul over the course of a day and night. The narrative then depicts an answer to this repentance as coming from a heavenly voice, either belonging to the Lord himself or some divine messenger, that declares explicitly that Enos has received *justification*: "thy sins are forgiven thee," the result of which is that Enos experiences his guilt being "swept away."[45] The salvific moment

---

43. I see the first verse in Enos as a sort of heading to his personal conversion story, in that it succinctly encapsulates the main elements of the conversion narrative that follows in verses two through eight. As a heading, I do not include it in my analysis of Enos's conversion proper.

44. See Benjamin Keogh's paper in this same volume.

45. Enos 1:5. As noted earlier, Enos's narrative is only one of two in which the moment of justification is enacted explicitly, such that the Lord specifically states that his sins are forgiven. The other is when we are told the people of Benjamin received a remission of their sins (Mosiah 4:3), although Alma subtly refers to the same thing when he relates that his soul was "snatched" from "eternal torment" with the result that his "soul is pained no more" (Mosiah 27:29).

proper ends with the declaration that his *faith* has made him whole, which constitutes him as a new being, *regenerated*. This regeneration is stated in terms ("wholeness") that can also connote a sanctified status regarding Enos's state of being. Like Alma$_2$ and other *Book of Mormon* believers, Enos's transformation to wholeness seems to be done in a moment, instantaneously in the very moment of justification.

Certain of these elements of Enos's conversion follow the same patterns as the other conversion stories in the *Book of Mormon*. For example, the words of Enos's father, which he recalled from memory but which he states explicitly that he had "heard," presumably through preaching, carry some kind of power in that they sink deep into Enos's heart and thus act as some kind of agentive force that begins the sequence of elements associated with the salvific moment.[46] Further, Like Nephi, Alma$_2$, king Lamoni, and Lamoni's father, the repentant Enos cries to God, and this crying extends through time. While he does not fall as if dead for three days and nights, he does cry mightily for a day and a night. In addition, like Alma$_2$, the guilt associated with his sins entirely disappears, in Enos's case being "swept away," while in Alma's case they were "remembered . . . no more." Finally, Enos's conversion is attributed, like the people of Benjamin, to faith in Christ.

The most obvious detail in which Enos's conversion narrative departs from the others is the fact that Enos's conversion uniquely takes place in the forest where he is all alone, in contrast to the many urban and communal settings in which conversion occurs in other *Book of Mormon* narratives. The reason for this difference is perhaps linked to the unsuccessful results of his own preaching (which is depicted later in the text)—there is no succession of cascading preaching on the part of those that might have been converted by his words. Thus, we are left

---

46. Enos 1:3. The words Enos remembers might be seen to be derived from a written text in addition to being transmitted through oral preaching. Three substantive discourses are associated with Jacob in earlier books prior to Enos's narrative. The first two are oral sermons given publicly to the people of Nephi 2 Nephi 6–10 and Jacob 2–3) but Jacob's third sermon was written instead of spoken (Jacob 4–6). However, the text of Enos's conversion explicitly states that he "remembered the words which I had often *heard my father speak*" (my emphasis), which for all intents and purposes seems to point to his father's oral sermons, not his written texts.

with his own sole conversion, away from the public eye and bereft of such revivalistic effects as many of the other narratives depict.

Enos's Second Preaching and the Perseverance of Records

Notwithstanding Enos's private conversion, physically distant from a public he could immediately turn to with a sermon of his conversion experience, we still see him enact the same impulse as other newly converted believers in the *Book of Mormon* who embark on a second iteration of preaching. Immediately following God's declaration that his faith has made him whole, Enos states that he "began to feel a desire for the welfare of my brethren the Nephites." However, instead of immediately embarking on a public preaching mission as we might expect him to do, we see him rather continue supplications to God in private prayer for the Nephites, pouring out his "whole soul" for them.[47]

The impetus for such a prayer is revealed in what immediately follows, and it has to do with what could be seen as the element of conditional perseverance, not regarding Enos himself but regarding his people the Nephites. In answer to Enos's prayer, the Lord presents a version of a conditional in terms of the fate of the Nephites. The Lord states, their fate will be decided "according to their diligence in keeping my commandments." This fate is located within the land itself. The Nephites will presumably prosper in the land *if* they keep the commandments, but the land itself will be cursed and the people will have "sorrow [brought] down upon their own heads" *if* they do not remain obedient.[48] Such language echoes the reminder for Nephi and the people of king Benjamin mentioned earlier, that their redeemed status is conditioned on their faithfulness in keeping the commandments, and it is consonant with the general impulse of the *ordo salutis* element of conditional perseverance. Enos seems to be worried that this conditional proposition will not end favorably for the Nephites. He seems convinced that *their* perseverance is not only not secure but seriously threatened.

---

47. Enos 1:9.
48. Enos 1:10

Enos's own personal perseverance seems to never be in question. He will remain as one whose sins are forgiven. But the question of the perseverance of his people looms large over the entire rest of the narrative, along with Enos's own personal response to such a worry, which in effect defers the familiar pattern of preaching-believe-preaching. Such a deferral constitutes another unique feature of Enos's narrative: the sequence of *believe* to the second *preaching* is interrupted by a series of prayers that ends in a bargain Enos makes with the Lord for the preservation of records.

Enos's bargain comes on the heels of his prayers for both the Nephites and the Lamanites, in response to the Lord granting him a fulfillment of his desires. Enos responds to such a gift from God by stating his deepest desire, "the desire which I desired of him," a statement that is again formulated as a conditional: *if* it should be that the Nephites fall into transgression and are thereby destroyed, *then* perhaps (and here is Enos's desire) God will preserve a record of their history that will then be made available to a future remnant of his people, represented by the surviving Lamanites. In short, Enos's desire is that the perseverance of the record will be the means of bringing salvation to future Lamanites. If the people themselves cannot be preserved, then the record can be preserved in their place. Presumably, this preserved/persevering record can then carry on the work of preaching necessary to carry forth the work of salvation, albeit through written texts but written texts that contain accounts of oral sermons and their salvific effects.

Enos's commitment to a written text as a tool of salvation has precedence in books that come before his, and indeed represents a theme that is to be seen both throughout the *Book of Mormon*'s narrative content and through the *Book of Mormon* as a material sign of this very preservation. For instance, it echoes Lehi's interest in the brass plates as a preserved record. Once Lehi became acquainted with the contents of the brass plates, he praises them as being of "great worth" because they will be the means to "preserve the commandments" to his posterity.[49] In other words, they are of great worth precisely as they function as a device of salvation. Jacob also states that his intent for his written text is

---

49. 1 Nephi 5:21.

for the purpose that "our children and also our beloved brethren" will know that "we knew of Christ."[50] Indeed, as a sort of proof text for this idea in a book that follows closely from Enos, the people of Zarahemla are presented as atheists with a corrupt language because "they had brought no records with them."[51] Enos's narrative shares in the same kind of valuation of a written record as a means for the saving of souls.

A preserved record is important enough to Enos that he again returns to the mode of crying unto God. Such a positioning of crying within the sequence of conversion is unusual when compared to the more formulaic aspects of other such *Book of Mormon* narratives, for crying is usually an action associated with the cries of the repentant to God. But here, such cries are made specifically for the sake of a preserved record. The faith he invokes here, not just after his cries of supplication but along with them—"I had faith and I did cry"[52]—is not just faith in Jesus Christ but in the covenant that Enos desires to make with God, a covenant in which he receives a promise that God will preserve the record. We see Enos, then, enact a similar pattern of supplication to God that he enacted for his own soul. Only now these cries are not coming from a repentant soul personally looking into the jaws of hell, but from a regenerate believer enacting a sort of proxy repentance for the sake of securing some modicum of perseverance for his people.

4. Conclusion

Once Enos finishes with these prayers and supplications, he then begins his oral preaching proper to both the Nephites and the Lamanites. However, unlike the other conversion narratives, his preaching seems to be done without much hope for its efficacy. As already noted, we see here no cascading motion of preaching-believe-preaching that carries through a line of the converted. We see only his somewhat bitter characterizations of the people who ignore his ministry. For whatever

---

50. Jacob 4:2–4.
51. Omni 1:17.
52. Enos 1:16.

reason his own oral words do not have the same kind of power to sink into the hearts of his listeners as the oral preaching of so many other *Book of Mormon* preachers. But even so, Enos's narrative offers a possibility that *written* words can carry on the preaching that must follow the salvific moment. The *written* record acts as an extension of the preaching that formulaically would follow from his status as a called, repentant, faithful, justified, and regenerated believer in Christ. Enos's spiritual investment into a written record that carries on preaching long after the preacher is gone thus constitutes an interesting innovation to the Book of Mormon conversion formula. This innovation designates the text as proxy to the preacher, and as such allows an almost unlimited reach of the preacher's words through time and space.

What can we make of the presence of this innovation in Enos's conversion narrative—that of a written text operating as proxy to the live, oral preaching that otherwise occurs as the final step in the *Book of Mormon*'s general pattern of conversion? I would argue it has to do, at least in part, with the idea that the book of Enos was quite possibly one of the very last books in the *Book of Mormon* to be transcribed and, as such, shows an acute awareness of the stated objective of the *Book of Mormon* as such. If we see the book of Enos as one of the last of the books to be transcribed, the fact of this narrative's clear echoes of the title page's claims for the objective of the *Book of Mormon* as a whole takes on greater contextual poignancy. The title page states that the *Book of Mormon* is a preserved record of primarily the Nephite people, "written to the Lamanites," with the express purpose of convincing readers that "Jesus is the Christ."[53] This language and intent are, of course, echoed in Enos's bargain with the Lord for the preservation of a Nephite record. In that latter case, the record was also meant to eventually find its way to a surviving remnant of Lamanites as a means of their conversion.

---

53. Granted, the language of the title page suggests a much broader scope of audience than just exclusively Lamanites. Nevertheless, the Lamanites as a "remnant of the house of Israel" are invoked throughout the title page's mention of "Jews" as well, and as such are conceptually included in that broader audience.

Granted, Enos's request could be seen as a prophecy of what will come in the course of the narratives that follow chronologically after his own. However, I see the order of transcription of the *Book of Mormon*, with Enos's book being one of the last to be finished, as an answer to the problem that the *Book of Mormon* actually ends with, that of the complete annihilation of the Nephites. By the time the book of Enos was completed, this annihilation was already solidified and enacted by the narratives that had already been transcribed before it. The book of Enos seems to assume that this destruction is a given for the Nephites, that is, that the conditions upon which a salvific perseverance is grounded, that of staying faithful by keeping the commandments, precisely will not and do not hold through time. In terms of explaining the unique features of Enos's conversion narratives when compared to the pattern established in other narratives, the idea that the book of Enos was transcribed almost nearly last thus has explanatory power. The book of Enos is preoccupied with the salvific role of a preserved record, the very record that the *Book of Mormon* itself claims to be. It seems reasonable to assume that Smith had the weight of this salvific role in mind as he completed the transcription process.

The answer to the problem of a Nephite failed perseverance that plays out in the book of Enos, the final books of the *Book of Mormon*, as well as on the book's title page is to offer a proxy to the one reliable source of calling believers forth: the orally preached word. Only now, with a written record that carries the narratives of such a means of external calling, this proxy will reach across time and space in ways that surpass the other conversion narratives' reach of the preached word. In this way, Enos's desire and covenant with the Lord to have a record persevere points to the concept of *The Book of Mormon* as an effort to gather a collection of conversion narratives, all of a piece in their formulaic character, in order that they may act collectively as a sort of *salutis* history. Enos's own personal conversion may be seen as the terminus to that collection before pivoting to secure, one last time, the actual perseverance of this collection precisely as a future tool for salvation.

Of Souls, Symptoms, and Supplements: Becoming Enos

Joseph M. Spencer

I TAKE AS A KIND OF SLOGAN for this paper a few words from Sigmund Freud, recognizing, of course, the risk I run in doing so. I think, though, that what Freud is getting at with the words I have in mind should be relatively uncontroversial. In a summary statement, he once famously wrote the following: *Wo Es war; soll Ich werden.*[1] Common English translations like "Where the id was, there the ego shall be" miss the force of Freud's German by imposing emerging technical language (not to mention the way that that translation obscures the normative force of *soll*).[2] What Freud says is this: Where it was, I must become. The idea here is that one does not emerge from the womb as a ready-made self, as a person in the fullest sense, *as an I.* Rather, the I *becomes.* And it does so, as Freud's taut formula suggests, some*where*, specifically at the site of something nonpersonal, there where *it* was.

Where it was, I must become.

---

1. Sigmund Freud, *Neue folge der Vorlesungen zur einführung in die psychoanalyse* (Vienna: Internationaler psychoanalytischer verlag, 1933), 111.

2. For the standard English text (which translates Freud's words as "Where id was, ego shall be"), see Sigmund Freud, *New Introductory Lectures on Psychanalysis*, trans. James Strachey (New York: W. W. Norton, 1965), 100.

It is with reference to this that I have chosen my subtitle: "becoming Enos." One of the many things on display in the familiar Enos story[3] found in the Book of Mormon is a minimally Freudian process of becoming—that is, of becoming-Enos. As for the title of my paper, it plays on a well-known talk given by Jeffrey R. Holland when he was president of Brigham Young University. He spoke "Of Souls, Symbols, and Sacraments."[4] I have playfully titled my essay "Of Souls, Symptoms, and Supplements." In doing so, however, I do not just mean to be cute. The three terms of my title outline what I hope to accomplish over the course of the paper. I will first say a word, by way of setting things up, about the idea of the soul—a key term in Enos's story. Second and less briefly, I will then identify two moments in the story where Enos's language becomes tortured—something I take to be a symptom, almost in the Freudian sense. Finally, before coming to a conclusion, I will reflect on how those two symptomatic moments in the story feature Enos's *becoming-I* against the backdrop of an impersonal *it*, as if the personal here supplements the nonpersonal.

Thus: of souls, symptoms, and supplements—by way of investigating what it means to speak of becoming Enos.

1. Souls

Anyone even passingly familiar with the Book of Enos knows the line with which the story turns to Enos's prayer: "and my soul hungered" (Enos 1:4).[5] The story thus begins with talk of the soul. And Enos goes on to speak relatively often of his soul. He offers his first prayer by way

---

3. Throughout this essay, I speak of Enos as a person, taking the autobiographical cast of the text just as it offers itself. I of course recognize other ways one might come at a text like this. But because the dawn of personhood encoded in Enos 1:1–18 is what interests me here, I take this approach throughout.

4. See Jeffrey R. Holland, *Of Souls, Symbols, and Sacraments* (Salt Lake City: Deseret Book, 2001).

5. For the text of the Book of Mormon, I use Royal Skousen, ed., *The Book of Mormon: The Earliest Text*, 2nd ed. (New Haven: Yale University Press, 2022), although I feel free to introduce punctuation of my own (rather than Skousen's) wherever it seems appropriate. On occasion, as well, I disagree with Skousen's conclusions regarding the

of "supplication for mine own soul" (v. 4). Later, when this prayer for his own benefit has yielded blessing and wholeness, he says, "I did pour out my whole soul unto God"—this time for his people, the Nephites (v. 9). And finally, after turning at last to pray for his enemies, the Lamanites, and after receiving divine comfort regarding their ultimate fate, Enos says, "my soul did rest" (v. 17).

As these data clearly show, if Enos's story is a story about anything, it is at least a story about a man's *soul*.

There are several ways one might gloss the choice of words here, the decision in the Book of Enos to speak of *souls* (to speak of souls at all, but also to speak of souls instead of using other at least semi-synonymous terms, such as *spirit*). For my purposes, however, I am interested in pursuing just one gloss on the word the text utilizes. In the King James Version of the New Testament—the style and diction of which saturate the English translation of the Book of Mormon[6]—the word "soul" universally translates the Greek word *psychē*, which becomes our word "psyche," referring to the mind.[7]

Now, I do not wish to leap foolishly from this bare lexical fact (about a Greek word from a highly determined and decidedly premodern context) to insisting that the Enos story concerns itself with the object of contemporary psychology (a thoroughly modern and materialist science). And yet there really is something of continuity here, something like a shared object of reflection. Enos does not plead with God for his heart or for his spirit, just as it is not his heart or his spirit that eventually rests.[8] It is another sort of thing that hangs in the

---

reconstruction of the earliest text; on all such occasions, this is noted clearly. Note also that all emphases in quotations from the Book of Mormon are my own.

6. On this feature of the Book of Mormon, see especially Nicholas J. Frederick, "The Book of Mormon and the Redaction of the King James New Testament," *Journal of Book of Mormon Studies* 27 (2018): 44–87.

7. Although "soul" always translates *psychē*, *psychē* and derivative forms are not always translated with forms of the word "soul." For instance, *psychikon* is rendered "natural" in key passages from 1 Corinthians 15.

8. Note that the words "heart" and "spirit" are not foreign to Enos—see verses 3 and 10—but that he does not choose to deploy these terms in speaking of what he struggles for and with.

balance as Enos recounts his prayers, and that thing is arguably Enos's very *person*. Thus, it seems to me, Enos's interest in his soul aligns well enough with my interest in the emergence of Enos's person against the backdrop of the nonpersonal to give me license to proceed.

I will, at any rate, take Enos's constant reference to his soul as motivation enough to pursue my proposed inquiry, my quasi-Freudian endeavor. My driving question is this: Where does Enos in his story present his soul or his person as coming into being?

2. Symptoms

In the seminar in which this paper had its origins, my fellow participants and I gave our full attention to the details of Enos 1:1–18, working on the text together for two full weeks. We asked questions like the following: How does Enos's story distribute its uses of "it came to pass," "behold," or "and now"? What should we make of this prepositional phrase in this verse or of that verb tense in that verse? Why does one bit of the text appear in direct quotation while another bit appears instead in indirect speech? Are there patterns that underlie Enos's uses of various titles for God? When does the pace of the narrative speed up or slow down, and when does one sequence of the story give way to another? Asking these kinds of questions over and over again, we developed a shared ear for this text.

With such an ear, we came to hear how straightforwardly Enos goes about telling his story, on the whole.[9] He moves through his narrative briskly, using "it came to pass" and other transitional formulas with a markedly low frequency for the Book of Mormon. He also seldom bends his story back on itself—that is, he mostly follows a clear chronological succession of events, which is also somewhat rare in the Book of Mormon. Further still, Enos's syntax is largely unbroken;

---

9. Kylie Turley argues elsewhere in this volume that verb tenses in Enos's narrative style constantly shift in peculiar ways. I am less inclined than she is to see the shifts in verb tenses as odd or unmotivated. For present purposes, though, this slight disagreement is immaterial. The straightforwardness of Enos's narrative style to which I refer concerns the pace of his storytelling above all else.

each subject generally has its verb, each prepositional phrase its place, each causal connective its motivation. Finally, Enos generally tends to avoid unnecessary language, rhetorical flourishes, throat-clearing words and phrases that do not change the basic sense of what he says. Enos is, one might say, a relatively undistracted storyteller, certainly by Book of Mormon standards. Naturally, there are dozens and dozens of questions worth asking about Enos's word choices, verb tenses, textual allusions, and so on. There is always plenty of grist for the careful reader's reflective mill! But at the level of simply lining up one event after another in syntactical prose, Enos seldom surprises.

Precisely for this reason, however, it is striking that, at just two moments in the flow of Enos's narration, the pace suddenly feels different. The difference is substantial enough, in fact, that someone well-accustomed to Enos's style cannot help but feel as if, at just those two moments in the story, she is not hearing *Enos's* voice. The unadorned style of narration falls away, and something else comes into focus. The two passages where Enos seems to take a hiatus are in this sense *symptomatic*, as I suggested at the outset of this paper. It is, of course, this pair of peculiar passages that draws my attention. For the remainder of this section of the paper, I will introduce them, putting off closer analysis until the next section.

The first symptomatic passage comes right at the outset of Enos's story, in verses 1–2. There, it seems, Enos has a hard time getting his story off the ground. What makes this clear is, above all, that the syntax of Enos's first sentence is broken as soon as it is begun, creating a grammatical problem that goes unresolved for so long that things begin to feel awkward. Verse 1 begins simply with "Behold, it came to pass that I Enos . . . ," but then the event these words introduce (Enos "went to hunt beasts in the forest") apparently does not show up

¹Behold, it came to pass that I Enos,

knowing my father, that he was a just man

(for he taught me in his language, and also in the nurture and admonition of the Lord—

and blessed be the name of my God for it!),

²and I will tell you of the wrestle which I had before God before that I received a remission of my sins—

³behold, I went to hunt beasts in the forest . . .

any earlier than verse 3.[10] In other words, as soon as Enos gets through "it came to pass that I Enos" in verse 1, he interrupts this first sentence with several lines about the figure he calls "my father" (verse 1) and a few words of direct address to his readers (verse 2). Only after all this—after four distracting or distracted lines in a row—does he finally get back to the event his initial "it came to pass that" introduces. Nothing like this kind of syntactical breakdown occurs elsewhere in Enos's story. It is a singularity, as well as a first symptom.

The second symptomatic passage comes much later in verse 13, at an odd moment when Enos unexpectedly interrupts the sequential flow of his story with a flashback. Before this point in his story (although things become somewhat more complicated afterward), Enos recounts things in the order they are supposed to have happened. At this point, however, Enos clearly begins to fill in backstory. After stating in verse 12 that he had prayed, and God had promised to grant him "according to [his] desires," Enos backs up in verse 13 to explain "the desire which [he] desired of [God]." But not only

[13]And now, behold, this was the desire which I desired of him: that if *it should so be that* my people, the Nephites, should fall into transgression and by any means be destroyed, and the Lamanites should not be destroyed, that the Lord God would preserve a record of my people, the Nephites— *even if it so be* by the power of his holy arm—that it might be brought forth some future day unto the Lamanites, that perhaps they might be brought unto salvation.

---

10. There are at least three possible ways of reading the odd syntax here. The one that makes the most sense to me—and thus that I assume here—is that verse 1's "it came to pass that" is meant to introduce the event that is finally reported at the outset of verse 3 but is interrupted by most of the content of verses 1–2. A second possibility (unpursued here) is that verse 1's "it came to pass that" is meant to introduce something extant within verses 1–2, perhaps "knowing my father," although the grammar employed in the text would then be (as Royal Skousen might say) non-standard. A third possibility (similarly unpursued here) is that verse 1's "it came to pass that" is simply abandoned at some point in verses 1–2, such that verse 3 does not resume the beginning of verse 1 but rather strikes out in a new direction—a syntactical breakdown that seems at least somewhat unlikely, although it is very possible. On the idea of "non-standard grammar" in the Book of Mormon, see Stanford Carmack, "The Nature of the Nonstandard English in the Book of Mormon," in Royal Skousen, *The History of the Text of the Book of Mormon, Part One: Grammatical Variation* (Provo, UT: FARMS and BYU Studies, 2016), 45–95.

does this create an atypical break in narrative sequence, it also comes accompanied by a clear uptick in prevaricating language, similarly uncharacteristic of Enos's narrative style. Two dimensions of verse 13 are especially interesting in this regard. First, Enos does not just say, as he clearly could and arguably would elsewhere in his story, "if my people the Nephites should fall into transgression"; rather, he writes, "if *it should so be that* my people the Nephites should fall into transgression." Second and similarly, Enos does not just hope that God would preserve a record "by the power of his holy arm," but more clunkily that he would do so "*even if it so be* by the power of his holy arm." Nowhere else in his story does Enos belabor his language in this fashion, using prevarications that add nothing to the sense of his words.[11] It is a second singularity, as well as a second symptom.

So far as I can tell, verses 1–2 and verse 13 constitute the only two strongly symptomatic moments in the whole of the story Enos tells about himself. They are, as it were, the only stylistic *hiccups* in his narrative. The question, though, is what these symptoms might tell us.

3. Supplements

How might the two just-discussed symptomatic moments in Enos's story operate (as I have been suggesting from the beginning) as two sites from which Enos emerges as a self? In the previous section, I have argued that what makes these moments unique within the narrative is their stylistic oddity, their being out of tune with the rest of the story Enos tells. But these two moments differ from the rest of the story in another way as well. They are unique also, that is, in that they constitute the only two moments in the narrative where something like becoming-a-self is on display. My wager here is the following: It is no coincidence that the two moments of stylistic peculiarity in Enos's

---

11. I use the word "sense" strictly here, according to the technical usage established by the logician Gottlob Frege. To say that the prevaricating phrases that uncharacteristically appear in verse 13 add nothing to the sense of the lines in which they are found is not to say that they add nothing to the aesthetic effect of the verse. For some introduction to these matters, see Gottlob Frege, "Sense and Reference," *Philosophical Review* 57.3 (May 1948): 209–30.

story (verses 1–2 and verse 13) are also the two moments where Enos-be-coming or I-becoming appears within the text. It is precisely this that I mean to signal by using the word "symptom." Enos's language becomes symptomatic precisely there where, and in that, his being—and there-fore his becoming-Enos—is at stake.

Why should narrative style break down when or where becoming-a-self is at issue in the text? The answer is obvious, albeit admittedly peculiar. The problem is this: How does one write personally about the pre-personal, the non-personal, or the super-personal? How does one write about the non-I or the non-self out of which one emerges as an I or a self? It is of course in no way impossible to write about such a thing, but to do so certainly requires a different sort of writing than straightforward narration.[12] In each of the two symptomatic passages in Enos's story, something non-personal irrupts within the otherwise personal narrative. So it is that, in Freud's terms, it seems most appro-priate at those moments to speak of an "it" that precedes Enos's "I." Where *it* was, *I* must become.[13] Each symptomatic passage thus (1) maps a nonpersonal field ("it") from which Enos emerges as a subject and (2) tracks Enos's coming into being ("I") against that backdrop.

My principal task in this section is to examine these two dimen-sions in turn for each of the two symptomatic passages in Enos's story. How might one describe the "it"—that is, the non-personal field—that appears in each of the narrative's *Wo Es war* moments? And what in turn is to be said about the "I"—that is, the emerging subject that is Enos—that shows up in each of the narrative's *soll Ich werden* moments? I will take up each of the two passages in turn.

---

12. So much of so-called "modern" art and literature—dominant for the first half of the twentieth century in Western letters—assumed baffling and alienating forms precisely because of their producers' interest in the question of the emergent self. Per-haps one way to speak of the symptomatic moments in Enos's story is that, ever so briefly, they mark "modern" moments in his narrative style, moments of baffling and alienating storytelling. For some interesting (but non-Freudian) reflection on this, see Michel Foucault, *The Order of Things: An Archaeology of the Human Sciences* (New York: Vintage, 1994), 303–43.

13. Verses 1–2 and verse 13 as loci constitute, one might say, the "where" of "Where it was, I must become," as applied to Enos 1:1–18.

Verses 1–2

As I have already noted, what is peculiar and symptomatic about verses 1–2 in the Enos narrative is the way they mostly function as an interruption. Verse 1 opens with "Behold, it came to pass that I Enos," but this thought goes unfinished until verse 3, when what "came to pass" is finally recounted: "Behold, I went to hunt beasts in the forest." The beginning of verse 3, after several lines of distraction, only eventually resumes the beginning of verse 1. This movements of suspension and resumption creates a syntactical oddity in the text that goes beyond mere distraction. It also splits—or at least doubles—the subject of the sentence. That is, the resumption of the interrupted thought, when it finally comes, repeats the grammatical subject of the suspended sentence: "Behold, it came to pass that *I Enos*. . . . Behold, *I* went to hunt beasts in the forest." Enos's "I" is from the start divided from itself, split in two and set at a distance from itself, fractured so deeply that most of verses 1–2 fall into the gap between a first "I" and a second "I."

What divides the self or the "I" here? What interrupts Enos as narrator the instant he says "I" and speaks his own name, "Enos"? Or rather, what occupies the space that separates one instance of "I" from the other within what is otherwise one and the same overarching sentence? The first answer that has to be given to this question is something Freud would certainly have smiled at. The interrupting lines of verse 1 are all about Enos's *father*.[14] "I Enos," he says, and he immediately has to add, "*knowing my father.*"

¹Behold, it came to pass that I Enos,

knowing my father,

that he was a just man

(for he taught me in his language,

and also in the nurture and admonition of the Lord—

and blessed be the name of my God for it!) . . . .

---

14. For Freud's classic and early formulation of the role he believed fathers play in psychic formation, see Sigmund Freud, *The Basic Writings of Sigmund Freud*, trans. and ed. A. A. Brill (New York: Modern Library, 1995), 274–79. For a substantial introduction to the issue of paternity in psychoanalysis as it was further and fascinatingly developed by Jacques Lacan, see Bruce Fink, *A Clinical Introduction to Lacanian Psychoanalysis: Theory and Technique* (Cambridge, MA: Harvard University Press, 1997), 79–111.

Enos, it seems, cannot begin to tell a story in his own name without interrupting himself—without putting his very self on hiatus—to bring his relationship with his father into focus. Enos's father-talk, moreover, comes in a cascade of five clauses that leads always further from the interrupted initial line. It's one thing for Enos to interrupt himself initially with "knowing my father," but then he somewhat awkwardly adds "that he was a just man"—a not entirely grammatical addition. As Enos continues, moreover, the awkward embellishments pile up: "for he taught me in his language," but then "and also in the nurture and admonition of the Lord," and finally and most interruptively, "and blessed be the name of my God for it!"

Each line subsequent to the first one in verse 1 contributes to the overarching interruption. Each line also interrupts its immediate predecessor. The result is that, by the time the reader comes to the end of verse 1, she is ostensibly reading an interruption of an interruption of an interruption of an interruption of an interruption of the sentence that starts way back at the beginning of the verse with "I Enos." Moreover, every interruptive line in verse 1 features Enos's tangle with his father. This cascading series of interruptive clauses sketches a map of the first *where* or the first *it* of Enos's narrative—the non-personal field where a first "I"-supplementation, a first becoming-Enos, might take place. And what is there before Enos shows up is, in a word, paternity. Enos emerges as a self only against the backdrop of his father's person, his father's character, his father's language, his father's providence, and his father's command.

Before verse 1's opening line is resumed at the outset of verse 3, verse 2 introduces a further delay. This further putting off of resumption, however, is of a wholly different nature from what precedes it in verse 1. Where the cascading clauses of verse 1 leave Enos's sense of self further and further behind while he maps the non-personal "it" from which he emerges, the further interruption of verse 2 finds Enos developing a rather startling sense of self. That is, after all the non-I father-talk of verse 1, verse 2 exhibits the *strongest* sense of self on display anywhere in the Enos story. "And I will tell you," Enos says, "of the wrestle which I had before God before that I received a remission of my sins." Not only does the first-person pronoun "I" appear here three times (and the first-person possessive pronoun "my" once) in a relatively short sentence,[15] but also the role played by this first-person speech in the Enos story is wholly unique. Only here does Enos say not just "I" but "you," addressing his readers with a second-person pronoun.[16] Verse 2 thus constitutes the only moment in the whole of Enos 1:1–18 where the pronoun "I" foregrounds Enos as *teller of* the story rather than Enos as *character in* the story.[17] It is in this sense that the selfhood or person that is on display in verse 2 is the strongest in the whole narrative.

The particularly strong sense of Enos's person that inhabits verse 2 emerges right against the non-personal (because paternal) field that stretches across verse 1. Verse 2 thus marks the "I"-supplement to verse 1's "it" and secures the first moment of becoming-Enos in the story. In fact, it is the coupling of verses 1 and 2 within one sustained interruption[18] that brings "it" and "I," *Es* and *Ich*, together. Only thus does the movement from the interrupted "I" of verse 1 to its resumption in verse 3 unfold in two key moments: that of "it" in verse 1, then that of "I" in verse 2. It in fact seems that the emergence of the "I" in verse 2 is crucial because it is this emergent "I" alone that proves strong enough to support the "I" of verse 3's opening line, resuming what was interrupted

---

15. One might initially wonder whether the several instances of "I" in verse 2 are resumptions of "I Enos" from the beginning of verse 1. But because the "I" of verse 2 announces what he *will* do, this "I" does not resume the "I Enos" that is attached in verse 1 to "it *came to pass.*" Verse 2 is a further interruption of verse 1's first line and a further delay of the ultimate arrival of verse 3's first line.

16. It seems significant that Enos is *addressed* in verse 1 ("my father . . . taught *me*"), while he is *addresser* in verse 2 ("I will tell *you*").

17. One could put this point this way: The uses of "I" in verses 1 and 3 function within the story, moving it along, but the uses of "I" in verse 2 function outside the story, talking about it.

18. It might be noted that the text would read just as smoothly if verse 2 were eliminated from the text. If verse 3 were to follow verse 1 immediately, however, the five interruptive clauses of verse 1 would map an "it" that is never explicitly supplemented with an "I," despite verse 3's first-person pronoun and its resumption of the pronoun at the outset of verse 1. Most of verse 1 would then feel like a simple parenthetical note about Enos's relationship to his father, rather than a symptom.

in verse 1. Enos comes (back) to himself, it seems, but only against the backdrop of the non-self of his paternal inheritances.

Wo Es war; soll Ich werden. Where it was, I must become.

Verse 13

After verse 3 resumes the interrupted first line of verse 1, Enos's generally uncomplicated style of storytelling proceeds at its apparently wonted pace until verse 13. For ten verses, Enos simply relates the tale of his wrestle before God without another grammatically suspicious break in the syntax of his sentences. Even when one comes to verse 13, where a new symptom arises, it is neither grammar nor syntax that is at issue. Instead, this new symptom takes the form of an uncharacteristically non-sequential bit of storytelling. Between verses 3 and 12, every event Enos recounts appears in what seems to be chronological order, such that the narrative flows smoothly and straightforwardly for a rather long time (at least, speaking narratologically). Until verse 13, the pace is even, and the reader feels as if she is receiving all the information she needs to Enos's experience. When verse 13 comes, however, Enos suddenly provides a few lines of flashback, filling in what suddenly appears retroactively to have been a gap in the story. Enos has already told of his prayer for the Lamanites in verse 11b and reported the consequent answer he received from God in verse 12, but verse 13 goes back to the prayer from earlier to make of it a fuller picture.

That Enos interrupts the sequentiality of his storyline might not be enough to give many readers pause. (Enos in fact seems to go on in several subsequent verses to trouble the sequential timeline of events in similar ways, as if the non-sequentiality of verse 13 makes it difficult for simple sequentiality to regain its footing for a few further verses.)[19] More important, however, is the fact that verse 13, uniquely within Enos's story, contains what I called above prevaricating language. The verse is weighed down with unnecessary and uncharacteristic phrases,

---

19. For some helpful structural analysis that makes sense of the sometimes-sinuous nature of the storyline in these later verses, see Benjamin Keogh's contribution to this volume. On Keogh's reading, it may be that verse 13 marks the only break in sequentiality in the story.

as if Enos is somewhat unsure about what he has to say in the verse. Ultimately, it is the prevaricating language that is especially interesting and symptomatic. Why should this flashback moment in Enos's story find him slipping out of his straightforward style of storytelling and into a more labored or even manneristic narrative style?

Verse 13 thus constitutes the second symptomatic moment in Enos's story. It does not concern the relationship between Enos and his father, but it is no less Freudian for that. Its subject is, explicitly, Enos's *desire*. The verse in fact opens with a double statement regarding desire; "this was the *desire* which I *desired*," Enos says. This little formula does much of the work that is of interest here. Of immediate importance is the fact that desire is split in two, divided from itself—in something like the way that the subject "I" divides in two in verses 1–3. The word "desire" is here first a noun with a definite article ("the desire"), as if desire were initially a thing all its own, outside or apart from any person. It thereafter immediately becomes a verb, however, one conjugated in the first person ("I desired"), such that desire next serves as something proper to somebody, as well as something eventual or even lived.

Divided from itself, desire as it features in verse 13 ("the desire which I desired") seems already to capture the kind of thing Freud had in mind with his formula, *Wo Es war; soll Ich werden.* The noun-form of "the desire" signals a non-personal "it," a "where" that serves as the location of becoming-I. In turn, the verb-form of "I desired" straightforwardly reports the becoming of the I that takes place against the background of the "it." Because verse 13 is given to explaining the structure of a desire that happened to become Enos's desire ("*this is the desire . . .*"), it can be said to sketch a map of the non-personal "it" that precedes Enos-as-self or Enos-as-subject.[20] But at the

[13]And now, behold, this was the desire which I desired of him: that *if it should so be* that my people, the Nephites, should fall into transgression and by any means be destroyed, and the Lamanites should not be destroyed, that the Lord God would preserve a record of my people, the Nephites— *even if it so be* by the power of his holy arm—that it might be brought forth some future day unto the Lamanites, that perhaps they might be brought unto salvation.

---

20. For an exposition of the complex topography of Enos's actual desire, as this is sketched in verse 13, see Adam Miller's contribution to this volume.

verse's beginning, there is also a claiming of this carefully mapped desire in an event of becoming-Enos (". . . *that I desired*"). The shift from "it" to "I" here has the grammatical form of a shift from the definite article ("the desire") to the first-person pronoun ("I desired").[21]

It is in verse 13's map of nonpersonal desire that the two prevaricating phrases to which I have already referred make their appearance: "it should so be that" and "even if it so be." It is worth noting right away that if one were to eliminate these two phrases from the text, every grammatical subject in verse 13's map of "the desire" would be genuinely substantial: "my people the Nephites," "the Lamanites," "the Lord God," "it" (referring to "a record"), and "they" (referring again to "the Lamanites"). Only in the two prevaricating phrases does any non-substantial subject appear. That is, in those phrases there appears what linguists call "empty" or "dummy subjects," two uses of "it" as grammatical subjects that do not seem to refer to anything.[22] What would the referent of "it" be in "if it should so be" or in "even if it so be"? Not only are these two phrases peculiarly verbose in the context of Enos's style of storytelling, but they also introduce a grammatical peculiarity into this verse, something otherwise uncharacteristic of it.

Perhaps the most natural reaction to the peculiarity just noted— the presence of dummy subjects in two stray phrases in verse 13—would be a shrug of the shoulders. What is the "it" of these two phrases but a trick of grammar?[23] I wonder, however, whether one should not in fact

---

21. That "the desire" is not Enos's alone is clear from the fact that God tells him in verse 18 that others have desired—or at least required—the same thing. It seems to me that this is what the depersonalizing definite article in "the desire" signals in its way. That desire is an "it," non-personal, although it might be claimed by persons such as Enos in gestures of self-constitution.

22. See, for instance, Rodney Huddleston and Geoffrey K. Pullum, *The Cambridge Grammar of the English Language* (New York: Cambridge University Press, 2002), 226: "Although complements usually correspond to arguments, there are some that do not. The clearest case is that of dummies, semantically empty [noun phrases] consisting of a pronoun and having a purely syntactic fashion." Such a pronoun "makes no independent contribution to the meaning of the clause," since the sense of the clause can be provided without it.

23. In many ways, the whole of twentieth-century philosophy as a project divided into its two overarching camps with respect to exactly this question. Martin Heidegger

sense in such dummy subjects precisely a hint of the non-personal "it" out of which the subject grows, a hint of the "it" that constitutes the site of I-becoming or Enos-becoming. There where Enos speaks of desire as if it had a life of its own ("*the* desire"), the occurrence and recurrence of a referentless "it" seems particularly appropriate. It is a grammatical subject with no personal subject behind it.

It is further interesting that both prevaricating phrases introduce *so-being* into verse 13: "it should *so be* that" and "even if it *so be*." It thus appears that the referentless "it"-subjects of the two phrases open directly onto a specific sort of being in each case: *so*-being, a sort of being where *its* being *thus* or *so* is (apparently) what is essential. The non-personal "it" that keeps arising in verse 13 apparently has a way it might (or "should") be, a "so" of its potential being. What these references to so-being trace is, rather explicitly, the twists and turns of the labyrinth of desire. There where Enos lacks control, "it" prevails by maybe being-so here, or maybe being-so there. Desire, it seems, tracks these possibilities. One might in fact note the uses throughout verse 13 of "if," "by any means," "might," and "perhaps," as well as the constant use of the subjunctive mood. These are all markers of possibility, and desire seems to track these possibilities while giving them a place ("it") and a form of being (so-being). And, of course, it is such a desire that Enos takes on in becoming-subject. This is, again, "the desire" that, he tells us, "I desired."

Wo Es war; soll Ich werden. Where it was, I must become.

---

laid many foundations for the so-called continental strain of twentieth-century philosophy by asking what philosophical significance might lie in just such an apparent trick of grammar. See Martin Heidegger, "What Is Metaphysics?" in *Basic Writings*, rev. ed., ed. David Farrell Krell (San Francisco: HarperCollins, 1993), 89–110. Carving out the rival space of the so-called analytic strain of twentieth-century philosophy, Rudolf Carnap insisted that such apparent tricks of grammar are of no philosophical significance whatsoever. See Rudolf Carnap, "The Elimination of Metaphysics through Logical Analysis of Language," in *Logical Positivism*, ed. A. J. Ayer (New York: Free Press, 1959), 60–81. For some helpful context and analysis, see Michael Friedman, *A Parting of the Ways: Carnap, Cassirer, and Heidegger* (Chicago: Open Court, 2000).

4. Concluding Reflections

I have argued here, in a slow teasing out of the text's possibilities, that Enos does not just tell a story about the progress of his prayers—from an initial concern about his own soul through an expanding sense of responsibility for others to the ultimate reception of a covenant about the Book of Mormon's coming forth. That is all there, of course, and it provides a template for rich devotional experience and much food for thought in its own right. But there is something else going on in the interstices of the text as well. At key points in the story, Enos lets his readers see how he first came even to *have* the soul that is at stake in his prayers. Whence this soul that hungers, that is prayed for, that is poured out, and that eventually rests? This soul is apparently something that has to be claimed, drawn out of something pre-soulish as the person who bears that soul comes into being. In Freudian terms, an "I" must supplement the tense and labyrinthine "it" that precedes it. Materialism could require nothing less.[24] And Enos's story features such a thing happening, it seems, at key symptomatic moments.

What, though, does all this reflection amount to? What conclusions might be drawn? Apparently, to wrestle soulfully before God cannot be a wholly *personal* thing. Enos insists on showing that, there where anyone might wrestle with (or even just before) God, far more than the would-be wrestler's person is at stake. This is apparently true in at least two ways.

First, the soul Enos finds himself bearing is something whose very substance—however subjectively shaped—is that of his father's language and nurture and admonition. He takes shape only against the background of his parents' interests and investments. So it is, though, that in every prayer, human relationships stretching back across generations are in play. "They without us should not be made perfect" (Hebrews 11:4). Each person who prays is therefore a bottleneck through which a long past finds expression before God. One who prays allows those before her to

---

24. Might all this be one way of glossing the peculiar passage to be found in Doctrine and Covenants 131:7: "All spirit is matter, but it is more fine or pure, and can only be discerned by purer eyes"?

hunger, to hunger in and through the soul she has forged from materials they have provided for her. They pray in her, wrestling with God.

Second, the soul Enos finds himself bearing is something whose very substance—again, however subjectively shaped—is that of a desire that weaves together so many ways the world might be. The fates of whole peoples (Nephites and Lamanites) trigger bone-deep desires that the world be thus or so, desires that precede Enos before they become something he identifies with in his own person. So it is, though, that in every prayer, networks of historical possibility, of possibilities that weave peoples together in a push for redemption, are always in play. "We without them cannot be made perfect" (D&C 128:18). One who prays allows the world's very demand for justice, for which she too struggles, to find a concrete expression for its rightful desire. All the world groans in her, requiring righteousness of God.

In short, when one wrestles and struggles and labors, giving bodily form to her soul's hunger and her heart's desire in prayer, multitudes cry out to God through the one who prays. There is no rest for the prayerful soul until or apart from the moment it can be said that what she has required is what others have required before her and will require after her. In prayer, one's soul becomes genuinely porous. Prayerful personhood takes shape only against the background of so many other praying persons, who in turn claimed themselves in prayer only against a similarly grander background of praying persons.

This is, after all, something Saint Paul says in his own way. And so, might I end with a few lines from Paul, rendered rather freely?[25]

> We don't know how to pray. When it's done right, however, something greater than us intervenes. You see, all of creation yearns to speak its pains and desires. And when we pray—given breath by what's greater than us—it's those pains and desires we express, right within ourselves.[26]

---

25. In a sense, I channel here the spirit of Adam Miller's paraphrases of scripture—and maybe in particular the spirit of his paraphrase of Paul's letter to the Romans. See Adam S. Miller, *Grace Is Not God's Backup Plan: An Urgent Paraphrase of Paul's Letter to the Romans* (n.p: Adam S. Miller, 2015).

26. See Romans 8, verses 22 and 26.

Re-reading: Enos, God, and Conversation

Benjamin Keogh

ENOS IS FAMOUS FOR WRESTLING IN PRAYER and in that way has become a model for a kind of perseverance in prayer that brings about the prayed for desire. What follows is an attempt to gently complicate that narrative. While Enos still emerges as a model of prayerful perseverance, he does so less self-assuredly. In contrast to the Enos who perseveres until blessings are secured from God in such a way that the conversation is stopped until the next time something is needed, at every turn the Enos that emerges here encounters a God who is intent on keeping the conversation going. On this reading it is not Enos's ability to get what he wants from God that makes him a model, but his continual acceptance of God's invitation to continue to communicate, even as he stumbles in the attempt. Despite his struggles, Enos remains. In this attempt, Enos is re-read as a cycle of four prayers and the language of "struggling/s" is investigated. But first, a word on God.

1. God and Conversation

There is, in the history of Christian theology, an understanding of God as an eternal conversation. Articulated by the Fathers, it was a prominent theme of Martin Luther's, and, most recently, it was taken up by the late German theologian Christoph Schwöbel. On this account "the Father is the Speaker, the Son the spoken Word, and the Holy Spirit the Listener who communicates what he has heard in the divine conversation to God's created conversation partners."[1] One of the implications of this, Schwöbel writes elsewhere, is that "all Christian theology has the character of conversation." Fundamentally, this is because Christian theology is rooted in in the conversational character of Christian faith "which is based in the practice of Christian faith as an ongoing conversation about God and with God." The conversational character of Christian faith, Schwöbel suggests, is itself "rooted in the fact that God engages in conversation with his creation, from creation until the consummation of God's conversations with his creation in the Kingdom of God." Further, the conversational character of God's engagement with creation "is rooted in God's own being as conversation so that the being of the world has its ground in the conversation that God is."[2] Understood this way conversation cascades from the conversation that God is, to the conversation that God has with God's creation, to the conversation that creation has with God which characterises Christian faith, to the conversation about God that characterises Christian theology.

On this way of framing things there is a certain sense in which Christian faith can be summed up in the practice of Christian prayer. This is so, perhaps, because undergirding the Christian practice of prayer is the belief that God is a personal agent who believers can communicate with and who can and will reciprocate by communicating with believers. In this way prayer becomes a fundamental site of expression for the act of fundamental trust in God that faith is. This is a key theme in Enos, albeit in a surprising way.

---

1. Christoph Schwöbel, 'The Eternity of the Triune God - Preliminary Considerations on the Relationship between the Trinity and the Time of Creation,' *Modern Theology*, 34:3, (2018), 335

2. Christoph Schwöbel, 'God as Conversation: Reflections on a Theological Ontology of Communicative Relations,' in J. Haers & P. De May (eds), *Theology and Conversation: Towards a Relational Theology*, (Leuven: Leuven University Press, 2003), 45.

2. Re-reading Enos

As a book, Enos clearly divides into two halves: an account of his prayers, followed by an account of the aftermath of his prayers. Here, our attention is solely on part one—the prayers—ranging from verse 1 to verse 18.

The first half itself quite neatly divides into five movements: an introduction, followed by four cycles of prayer—the last of which concludes by returning to and clarifying the introduction.

Similarly, each of the four prayer cycles divides quite nicely into four parts:

    i.   a motivating factor for the prayer
    ii. a prayer
    iii. a response
    iv. a resolution to the cycle[3]

For prayers one and four this four-part cycle is fixed. For prayers two and three the cycle is more porous with part iv. of the second cycle also functioning as part i. of the third cycle. Together this works to link cycle one with cycle four, and cycle two with cycle three.

Enos' four prayer cycles can be conceived as follows:

1. A mighty prayer for his own soul, characterised by hunger
2. A pouring out of his whole soul for the Nephites, characterised by struggle
3. A prayer of diligent labour for the Lamanites, characterised by many long strugglings
4. A continual prayer for the records, characterised by faith.

The use of struggle in the characterisation of prayers two and three link them together, while faith in prayer four replaces hunger in prayer one. Together these give the suggestion of a chiastic structure to the first

---

3. While articulated differently, my articulation of the four-foldedness of each prayer cycle is indebted to Joseph Spencer's. My thanks to him and the rest of the seminar participants for the conversations that made this piece better.

half of Enos's book: the cycle is bookended by the introduction and the resolution to prayer cycle four which functions as a resolution to the movement as the whole; and it finds its centre in the porous line that ends cycle two and begins cycle three.

With that much clear, a word on each of the five movements in an attempt to add some meat to these bare bones.

Movement 1—Introduction (vs. 1–2)

The introduction does two things. First, it situates Enos in relation to his father, and second, it situates Enos in relation to God. That the reported situation of Enos in relation to God in the introduction as having received a remission of his sins is only fully realised as the first half of the book is coming to an end suggests two things: first, that Enos's reception of a remission of his sins is worked out over the course of the whole four-prayer-cycle; and second, that the situating of Enos in relation to his father—his knowing that he was a just man—is likewise a result of the whole four-prayer cycle. Said differently, Enos does not enter into prayer because he reasoned his father was a just man—he reasoned his father was a just man because he entered into prayer.

Movement 2—First Prayer Cycle (vs. 3–8)

If the introduction reports the relational situation of Enos *after* his encounters in prayer, the first cycle reports his relational situation *before* his encounters in prayer. First, as a human in the image of God Enos is the inheritor of humanity's original address from God yet as he begins his story instead of exercising creative care over God's creation, Enos is hunting it with the intent to destroy some part of it. Dislocated in his relationships Enos is in a state of disrelation with God's creation. Second, the suggestion that he repeatedly heard his father's words without *hearing* them—it is only on the hunt that they begin to sink into his soul—suggests Enos's dislocation in relation to others and thereby his disrelation with them. This situation is confirmed in later cycles in relation to both Nephite and Lamanite others. Third, the experience of hunger and the need to petition God "for mine own soul" (vs. 4) suggests a dislocation in Enos's relation to himself. And fourth, the pronouncement of forgiveness of sin that underlines Enos's need for forgiveness demonstrates his dislocation in relation to God.

Enos, in other words, is an inheritor of the common human condition. Creation by God *locates* humans not just in a specific relation to God, but in an ordered relation to themselves, to other humans, and to the rest of God's creation. In this way invocation of the Fall is an expression of humanity's disrelation in each of these relationships which reveals their interlinking: disrelation with God entails disrelation with oneself, other humans, and the rest of God's creation. Said differently, *dislocation* in one relation dislocates one in all relations. Here is revealed the difference between God—who exists eternally in an infinite state of unbroken relational communion between the Father, Son, and Spirit which spills out into everlasting loving relations with all that is not God—and humans whose finite existence is characterised by relations that continually break. Because human relations continually break the relational *relocation* of humanity requires an act of God. This is what atonement expresses.

It may be that Enos's first prayer grows out of his dawning realisation of this situation. The prayer itself, however—"for mine own soul"—seems to lack a specific objective. While his hunger implies lack, Enos does not specify the lack his prayer is trying to address. In response an unidentified voice that Enos attributes to the Lord announces forgiveness of sins and the cycle rounds out with an explanation that faith in Christ has made Enos "whole" (vs. 8).

Movement 3—Second Prayer Cycle (vs. 9–11)

Beginning to feel a desire for the Nephites' welfare, Enos acts that desire out in prayer by pouring out his freshly whole soul for them. Rooting the prayer in a generic desire for Nephite *welfare* makes this cycle slightly less objectiveless than the first, in which Enos's concern for his own soul was unqualified. In response a voice came to Enos's mind, that he described as the Lord's, and it explained life in relation to God. When commandments are kept—which is another way of saying when relations are right—humans experience God's love as love. When relations are not right, it will be evident in humanity's interactions with the land and humans will experience God's love as wrath. In both instances God's love is doing the same thing: inviting humans into further communion with God. The different experience of God's love as love and God's love as wrath is therefore not because there is a difference in God's expression, but because the relational stances of humans are different. In response Enos describes his faith as beginning to be "unshaken in the Lord" (vs.11).

It is this line about unshaken faith that functions both as the resolution of the second cycle, and as the motivating factor for the third. It connects not only the two prayers, but the narrative as a whole, and perhaps in this way, is a key to the text. Leaving discussion of this possibility and Enos's description of his faith "[beginning] to be unshaken" until later, a word for now on faith itself.

As this porous line suggests, faith is passively constituted in a person and actively received by that person. A person cannot generate faith because faith is dependent upon a disclosure event from God that is authenticated for the person by God. As an event of illumination, it reorients a person in their relations with God, themselves, other persons, and the rest of God's creation because it discloses reality's true character as determined by God's action in creation, reconciliation, and perfection. This Enos has experienced in forgiveness of sin and sweeping away of guilt, and now in his reception of the Lord's word about the nature of reality. As with Enos, it is the active acknowledgement of this passive disclosure that initiates the faith-filled into a life of faith in which the divine work of faith's constitution becomes the fundamental orientation for a person's actions. In this way faith can be described as "the act of fundamental trust in God which is the active acknowledgement of the truth of God's revelation as it is passively disclosed for the believer"[4] which in its reorienting of a person's relation to reality becomes the structuring principle of reality and provides the fundamental orientation for subsequent action. In this way the *constitution* of faith is understood as the work of God and the *practice* of faith as the defining characteristic of the believer. In this way while faith—as it was for Enos—is passively constituted for the believer by

---

4. Christoph Schwöbel, *God: Action and Revelation*, (Kampen: Pharos, 1992), 128.

God, the believer's acknowledgement and acceptance of the disclosure as the orienting principle for their life means that faith can properly be called—as it was by Enos—the believer's own.

Movement 4—Third Prayer Cycle (vs. 11–14)

Here, a slightly longer word.

As the motivating factor for the third cycle, it is Enos's description of his faith as beginning to be unshaken in the Lord, rather than any stated desire for the Lamanites, that turns his attention to the Lamanites. This turning demonstrates not only that faith becomes the fundamental orientation for all of a person's actions, but that in becoming so it opens up new possibilities for human action and thereby re-constitutes that person's role as an agent in the world. Its outworking in the third prayer cycle however, makes clear that in practice the process is not straightforward.

On its face prayer three appears objective, even if complicatedly so. However, the upshot—a request that in the event that the Nephites are destroyed and the Lamanites are not that a record of the Nephites would be preserved by God that "might" at "some" point "perhaps" (vs. 13) bring salvation to the Lamanites—has a remarkably objective-less quality to it. It is also relationally weak. This may be a function of its origin in Enos's new way of acting in the world which appears to comprise the attempt to transfer the Nephite struggle to restore the Lamanites to "the true faith" (vs. 14) onto God.

Outside of Enos the word struggle, or one of its cognates, appears seven times in the Book of Mormon. Here they are laid out:

> Mosiah 7:18   "our many strugglings, which have been in vain" / "I trust there remaineth an effectual struggle to be made"

> Alma 27:1   "those Lamanites who had gone to war against the Nephites had found, after their many struggles to destroy them, that it was in vain to seek their destruction"

> Mormon 2:14   "they would struggle with the swords for
> their lives"
>
> Mormon 5:2   "they did struggle for their lives without
> calling upon that Being who created them"
>
> Mormon 6:6   "the last struggle of my people"
>
> Ether 15:31   "after he had struggled for breath, he died"

In each instance, not only was the struggle lost, the thing against which the struggler was struggling ultimately overcame the struggler. Limhi's people fell deeper into bondage. The warring Lamanites lost more Lamanites. Mormon's people died. Shiz ran out of breath. The one outlier, perhaps proves the rule. Limhi's assertion that there remained an "effectual struggle" which would result in their freedom proved incorrect. Rather than gaining freedom through struggle, the Nephites walked out while the Lamanite camp was asleep and gained their freedom without a struggle. Outside of Enos then, struggles not only fail, they result in the thing against which the struggler was struggling ultimately overcoming the struggler. The pattern holds for Enos's Nephites: not only did their struggle to restore the Lamanites to true faith fail, it resulted in a hatred that was fixed. In the struggle to control the Lamanites, agency was ceded to the Lamanites, with their swearing in their wrath to destroy the Nephites and their records placing the Nephites in a position where their efforts were spent avoiding the sworn destruction.

Repetition of struggle in relation to Nephite efforts and Enos's prayer links the two, while the details of each make clear that Enos's transference of the Nephite struggle to God is complete. In the prayer true faith is functionalised as Nephite faith; the fulfilment of Lamanite wrath in Nephite destruction is conditionalised but also separated and made incomplete in the request for the preservation of Nephite records; and the eventual re-imposition of Nephite superiority (lost in the struggle to bring the Lamanites to Nephite faith) through the records bringing the Lamanites to Nephite faith is enjoined, if weakly—maybe, perhaps, at some point.

That this prayer is not prayed out of Enos' desire for the Lamanites, but is instead rooted in the unshaken faith Enos' reports himself as beginning to develop as a result of the response to his prayer for the Nephites is suggestive. So too is the response: "the Lord said . . . I will grant unto you according to thy desires, because of thy faith" (vs. 12). This, it seems, is a succinct restatement of the response to prayer two. If faith is understood as the act of fundamental trust in God, then faith is an expression of one's relational posture in relation to God and that relational posture will underpin and, in many ways, determine not only the experience of God, but of ourselves, of others, and of God's creation. Put more bluntly, in response to Enos's relationally weak prayer, God asks, "what kind of relations do you want?"

If repetition of struggle links Enos's prayer and Nephite efforts in relation to the Lamanites, then its repetition in relation to the prayers in the second and third cycles links the two cycles—and it is this, perhaps, that suggests why this porous middle line about "unshaken" faith that cements the connection of the two is a key to the text. In every other instance the one engaged in a struggle not only loses the struggle, but is overcome by what they are struggling against. Here, God does not overcome Enos. Instead, God attempts to recalibrate the relationship by redirecting and thereby reimposing Enos's own created freedom. One way this may be evident is in Enos's reporting of God's words where God attributes God's response to Enos's faith and not to Enos's prayer. By keeping the conversation going God invites Enos to continue conversing. By accepting the invitation Enos remains in relation. If faith is "the act of fundamental trust in God" that can be summed up in the practice of Christian prayer then Enos's continuation in prayer is a decision for faith. In this way, perhaps, the strangeness of this central middle line—"my faith began to be unshaken in the Lord" (vs. 11)—can be explained as Enos's attempt to express and integrate his continuing realisation of faith's passive constitution with his continuing determination to actively receive faith as the structuring principal of his reality which provides the fundamental orientation for his future actions. Despite the struggle, Enos is determined to remain in conversational relation. If this is the case there is a surprising implication: unshaken faith is itself porous. Like the line that completes cycle two and kicks off cycle three thereby cementing their connection, unshaken faith as the determination to stay in conversational relation with God must be permeable—able to withstand the give and take of conversation yet remaining immovably in relation with God.

Movement 5—Fourth Prayer Cycle (vs. 15–18)

Enos begins cycle four with a gloss on the Lord's response in cycle three. A charitable reading suggests Enos understands that because faith is an act of fundamental trust in God then the act (or lack) of faith expresses one's relational posture towards God. Read this way asking and receiving in faith aims at and brings about fuller communion with God, one's self, other humans, and the rest of God's creation. Less charitably, Enos interprets God's response legalistically: the agreement is, with the right amount of faith and the right kind of belief one can get whatever one asks for. On the basis of prayer four deciding between the two is difficult. Again the prayer is a result of Enos' faith—although this time stripped of association with unshakenness and struggle. On the one hand the "I had faith, and I did cry" (vs. 16) formula may be suggestive of an understanding of faith as an expression of one's relational posture towards God which naturally flows into communication with God through prayer. On the other, it is suggestive that the words of this prayer strip prayer three of its relational content and straightforwardly asks for the preservation of "the records" (vs. 16). In response God reinserts the relational dynamic, cements the relation with a covenant, and Enos finally rests.

3. Conclusion

In conclusion, three final comments.

First, remaining in the conversation intensified Enos's experience of God. This is evident across the four prayer movements as the responses progressed from an unidentified voice, to a voice identified with the Lord, to the Lord unqualified by voice, to God who covenants. As the conversation who invites conversation God's responses to Enos have kept the conversation open and by accepting the invitation to further conversation Enos has moved toward God. Because the development of unshaken faith expresses the determination to stay in conversation and because covenant expresses God's commitment to the conversation, Enos can continue—even if in the future he experiences the conversation as less than intense and God feels silent.

Second, that Enos's rest is a response to covenant reveals that his rest is a reconciliation, not a cessation. The second half of the book immediately begins with Enos out among the people and the conversation with God inevitably continuing. It is here, however, as the movements conclude that Enos's story of receiving a remission of his sins finally finds fulfilment. Covenant. Rest. Remission. Reconciliation. The introduction of the fathers at this point expands the field of Enos's relating. Understanding "required" (vs. 18) here as "made necessary" and not "demanded" suggests that it was the fathers' unshaken faith, expressed in their determination to remain in conversation, that led to their reception of covenant. Knowing they experienced what he had, Enos knew his father was a just man.

Third, and finally—covenant, it becomes clear is not about binding God to a legal agreement that transforms prayer into a means of enforcing its terms or claiming its benefits. Instead, covenant expresses a relational relocation. Thus relocated one not only sees the world in a new way but can now act in new ways in relation to God, oneself, other humans, and the rest of God's creation. In this way Enos, despite, and yet in many ways because of his struggles, has found a more excellent way—and all it requires is participation.

Hungering and Hunting for Enos and the Missing Words

Kylie Turley

> "And to Seth, to him also there was born a son; and he called his name Enos: then began men to call upon the name of the Lord."
>
> Genesis 4:26

ENOS'S STORY SHOULD BE EASY. After Nephi and his love of Isaiah, and Jacob and his lengthy, multiple-day sermons, Enos seems understandable. He's just a hunter who talks to God, a regular guy who prays long enough to receive some solid revelation. And yet careful readers are squirming with discomfort by the middle of Enos's first sentence: Enos declares that he knows his father, Jacob, was a just man—and then fades off into distracted subordinate clauses about Jacob, his language, and his nurturing and admonishing. The sentence is written with enough poetic flare that many readers are thoroughly sidetracked, effectively forgetting where Enos began and thus overlooking the fact that the sentence never ends. Enos's sentence is left hanging and disconnected. His story is missing words.

And that is just the first of many questions and gaps in this narrative. Enos's story begins by stumbling over a few images and then by setting those images within a disjunctive plot. Enos says he is going to tell "you" of the "wrestle" he had "before God" (Enos 1:2). What is this wrestle? With whom is he wrestling? And why does he abruptly switch metaphors from wrestling to hunting beasts? Why *beasts*? Why *hunting*? The questions continue when readers stumble out of Enos's metaphoric forest and into a story with some chronology issues: is this one long wrestle-prayer that spans one long day (and night)? Or is this a wrestle-prayer metaphor that spans the day of Enos's entire life until the "night" of his "rest"/death? What happens and when does it happen? Which words are the words that sink into hearts? Do readers notice that they never learn how the story ends? What happens on the hunt?

Mining the text for answers is helpful, but linked images and word echoes make comparison an appropriate technique. Overlaying Enos's prayer narrative (Enos 1:1–18)[1] with Psalm 42 and Psalm 43 (Psalm 42/43)[2] creates a site of productive tension with multiple points of contact. This paper approaches Enos's story through these points of contact, comparing overlapping words and images as a method to uncover meaning (or lack of meaning) within Enos's story. This essay will address the overlapping images or word "echoes,"[3] focusing on the

---

1. I am considering Enos 1:1–18 to be Enos's "prayer narrative."

2. Given their nearly identical refrains and Psalm 43's lack of a superscription, I will consider the text of Psalm 42 and Psalm 43 to be one psalm, similar to many modern, non-KJV versions of the Hebrew Bible. They constitute the introduction to the Korahite Psalms, which include Psalms 42–49, 84–85, and 87–88.

3. These linked phrases fall short—at least initially—of being labelled as full-fledged "allusions." I will refer to them as word "echoes," which are the lightest of references on Nicholas J. Frederick's four-tiered system of allusivity. I will also refer to them as "images" due to their engagement of imagination and sensory perception. See Nicholas J. Frederik, *The Bible, Mormon Scripture, and the Rhetoric of Allusivity*. (Lanham, Maryland: Fairleigh Dickinson University Press, 2016), xxviii–xix. Numerous studies in the last few decades have noted quotations and allusions to the psalms in various Book of Mormon texts. These efforts have yielded lists of apparent psalm quotations, as well as not ungrounded accusations of "parallelomania." (See, for example, Douglas F. Salmon. "Parallelomania and the Study of Latter-day Scripture: Confirmation, Coincidence, or the Collective Unconscious?" *Dialogue: A Journal of Mormon Thought* 33, no. 2 (2000): 129–156.) It is not my aim to suggest or to prove a verifiable, historical, extratextual reliance connecting Enos's narrative and Psalms 42/43. My overlay of Psalms 42 and 43 is more of a literary-theological experiment than a historical argument. It is also

introductory animal images, ongoing prayer that occurs before God, crying to the Lord day and night, and souls that hunger, thirst, and occasionally pour out. These images and words connect Psalm 42/43 and Enos's narrative, and they do so in ways that define each better before branching out into issues of context and setting, timing and efficacy of prayer, and individual identity formation. As Ben Hutchinson notes in his 2018 Oxford University Press contribution to the Oxford's Very Short Introduction Series, "comparative close reading . . . examin[es] the ways in which the micro-analysis of textual detail can open up the macro-analysis of contextual significance."[4] When pressed by comparison, Enos's narrative displays a surprising pattern of incomplete imagery and plot dysfunction, coalescing around Enos, a character who turns out to be surprisingly empty and disconnected. He is hunting for beasts, and he is hungry—probably for his missing people, for his God, and possibly for his own soul. Ironically, even while comparison displays Enos's disconnection and relative emptiness, it is also the key that links Enos to his past—allowing him to see what actions are needed to fill his emptiness and reconstitute his present and his future with relationships that matter.

---

not a form critical argument. Though I refer to scholarship that situates Psalm 42/43 as a lament, I am not arguing that Enos's narrative has a particular form or should be labelled as a particular genre. Because this is more of a literary-theological experiment and dating is not of particular concern, I will not spend undue effort proving the possibility, availability, and/or probability of an intertextual relationship. I will simply note the following: in an 1800s context, the psalms were, of course, widely available. Many theologians, philosophers, and other academics argue that thematically, the first three psalms of Book 2 of the Psalter (Psalms 42, 43, 44) make most sense when read as literature of exile, yet scholars have dated these first three hymns of the sons of Korah ranging from eighth century BCE to the second century BCE, meaning that they could have been available and known to Lehi, and clearly were known by and available to Joseph Smith. This is a literary reading. As such, I consider the text in its current state.

4. Ben Hutchinson, *Comparative Literature: A Very Short Introduction* (Oxford, Oxford University Press, 2018), 26.

1. A Hart, Beasts, and a Heart

Psalm 42/43 begins with a "hart" that "panteth after the water brooks" (Psalm 42:1). Through incremental changes, the psalm first replaces the deer with the psalmist's soul and the flowing, life-giving water of the brook with God. Around the verb, "panteth," the first and second clauses use phrasing that produces a simile: "as the hart panteth after the water brooks/so panteth my soul after thee, O God" (Psalm 42:1). The simile compares the hart and human, as well as living, moving water and God. Both hart and human "pant," suggesting an almost animalistic need or desire for their respective object: the deer longs for water and the psalmist longs for God. The next poetic line changes the verb: "My soul thirsteth for God, for the living God" (Psalm 42:2), which completes the transformation. The change in verb changes animal panting to human thirsting, but it does so only after a primal seeking for God—a desperate longing as strong as a physical need—has been established. This is the symbolic "thirst" that the poet has for God.

Enos's story also begins with need and with an animal, but his narrative seems less poetic and less perceptive because it is more generalized. Verse three simply states that Enos "went to hunt beasts in the forests" (Enos 1:3). Taken at face value, the words connote Enos's need for food and the actions necessary to remedy that need. That situation connects Enos with his uncle, Nephi, who also went "slay wild beasts," though Nephi did so in the old world and with more dire physical circumstances. Faced with his own and his family's starvation, Nephi armed himself with a homemade bow, journeyed to "the top of the mountain," and there he "did slay wild beasts" (1 Ne 16:30, 31). Within a context of family and hunger, Nephi apparently hunted and then slayed beasts. Enos similarly invoked family with his reference to his father in the first sentence, but he says he hungers in verse 4, which is after he went to hunt beasts in verse 3. Nephi's hunt is more desperate and his desire more urgent, since failure means his family will "perish in the wilderness with hunger" (1 Ne 16:35). Enos does not seem to particularly care about the hunt, easily shunting it aside (and never returning to it) when his father's words sink into his heart.

Besides the mere existence of introductory animal imagery, it may seem as if there is little connection between Enos's beasts and the psalmist's hart. The psalmist's hart was likely "swift and fleet of foot" and located "in high places" such as mountaintops,[5] but Enos's hunt is in the "forests" of the new world. Bridging the gap is Nephi, someone who has slain wild beasts (such as those that Enos is hunting for) in the top of the mountain (such as those the psalmist's hart would live in). There is no immediate reason to think Enos is hunting for any reason besides hunger or pleasure, while the psalmist's hart is obviously symbolic.

The actions of the hart are described using third person, feminine singular verbs. In *Psalms, Books 2–3*, Denise Dombkowski Hopkins analyzes the text on a word-level and concludes, "Because these verbs are third person feminine singular in form, we would expect the feminine singular noun for deer (doe), to correspond."[6] Arthur Walker-Jones, citing work by Dahood and H.I. Ginsberg, argues for a text emendation, though he concludes that even without emendation, "the verb makes clear that the subject is feminine."[7] The insinuations are fascinating: the first few verses establish the comparison of hart with psalmist. Metaphorically-speaking, the hart is the psalmist. If this hart is a female deer, then the speaking "I" in Psalm 42/43 may also be a woman. Melody Knowles' work on a possible woman psalmist/author of Psalm 131 reminds the reader that there are other possibilities. In "A Woman at Prayer: A Critical Note on Psalm 131:2b," Knowles explains that even if all agree on "the identification of a female voice in this text," there could be multiple reasons for that voice. Female authorship is, of course, one possibility, though the text might also be an extended quotation of a woman or the work of a creative author depicting the speaking voice of someone else or simply a metaphor, since "metaphors

5. Arthur Walker-Jones, *Psalms Book 2: An Earth Bible Commentary: "As a Doe Groans,"* (London: Bloomsbury Publishing, 2019), 56. See, especially, footnote 17.

6. Denise Dombkowski Hopkins, *Wisdom Commentary: Psalms, Books 2–3 (42–89)*, Reid, Barbara E., Elisabeth Schüssler Fiorenza, and Mary Ann Beavis, eds. Wisdom Commentary Series, vol. 21. Liturgical Press. (2016): 7.

7. Arthur Walker-Jones. *Psalms Book 2.*

are not strictly confined to the experience of the author."[8] What is clear
is that the hart's actions are constructed as feminine, singular verbs.
Some scholars suggest this is reason enough to assume that the hart
is actually a hind (female deer). The KJV translation uses the noun,
hart, although most modern versions, including the New King James
Version,[9] use the non-gendered *deer* rather than hart or hind (or doe).

Whether a hind or a hart, the symbolic deer in Psalm 42/43 is
thirsty. Alexandra Pesch explains that deer have for millenia "play[ed]
a role in the symbolism of the sun, until they even appear as symbols
of Christ in the Middle Ages." That symbolism also ties into the widespread belief that deer could locate "snakes with their snorting, pull
them out of their holes and devour them." This tradition insisted that
"the snake's poison . . . could not harm [the deer] as long as they drink
fresh water promptly after eating." Pesch ties this tradition to the deer
in Psalm 42/43, suggesting that this tradition is evident in the deer's
thirst for the water and the living God.[10]

The figurative language regarding the meaning of the hart weighs
on Enos's narrative and draws similar, less literal language to the surface. Like the hart, Enos's "heart" is used figuratively. Enos says his
father spoke words about eternal life and these words "sunk deep in to
[his] heart" (Enos 1:3). Of course, words cannot sink into someone's real
heart. But if there were ever words that were going to do so, it might be
these ones. They seem almost willful. Notably, Enos does not say that
he recalled the words, that he pondered them, or that he opened his
heart to them. It seems as if the willful words decided to come into his
mind and sink themselves into his heart.

If words have some sort of agency in Enos's estimation, if they
can act for themselves, then Enos's narrative becomes slippery and

8. Melody D. Knowles, "A Woman at Prayer: A Critical Note on Psalm 131: 2b,"
Journal of Biblical Literature 125, no. 2 (2006): 385–389

9. See Bible Hub. "Psalm 42:1." Accessed October 27, 2022. https://biblehub.com/
psalms/42-1.htm

10. Alexandra Pesch, "A Hind to Your Health!" In *Small Things–Wide Horizons:
Studies in Honour of Birgitta Hårdh*, edited by Lars Larsson, Fredrik Ekengren, and
Bertil Helgesson (Oxford: Archaeopress Publishing Ltd, 2015). http://www.jstor.com/
stable/j.ctvr43jxs.24

unpredictable. Attention must be focused on the words because much of what happens to Enos occurs as a response to words. Hearing the Lord's words about Christ and his "faith . . . mak[ing] him whole" cause Enos to "be[gin] to feel a desire for the welfare of [his] brethren" (Enos 1:9). Hearing the "voice of the Lord" in his "mind" promising to "visit [his] brethren according to their diligence" (Enos 1:10) provokes Enos's faith to "be[gin] to be unshaken" (Enos 1:11). And, finally, Enos is able to "rest" (Enos 1:17), after the Lord "covenanted with [him] that he would bring [the records] forth unto the Lamanites" (Enos 1:16). Words are a critical component of cause and effect. They are desire-impacting, action-producing, and emotion-changing initiators.

Problematically, Enos's narrative leaps over connective words, skips explicit comparison-inducing language, and moves from hunting beasts to the hunger of his soul. Were Enos to follow the pattern of symbolism in Psalm 42/43, his story would be much more obviously symbolic, replete with visual images and iteratively-constructed metaphors. Instead, Enos interacts with his exterior world through a moment of hunger and perhaps through physical engagement in hunting, wrestling, and kneeling, actions that are conceivably symbolic. Whether those actions are symbolic is debatable.

Other than those moments, Enos engages his world almost exclusively through aural/oral (hearing/speaking). If one reads this story on an entirely literal level, the dearth of visually-oriented imagery could mean that Enos is blind. Ironically, the assumption that Enos is alone, hunting for beasts in the forests in the land of Nephi blinds us to the fact that there is virtually no visual imagery in Enos 1:1–18. If one reads this story symbolically, then the power of Psalm 42/43's iterative movement would be helpful. It could connect the images of hunting and beasts and forests and hunger. Instead, readers have to navigate a huge leap from "I went to hunt beasts in the forests" (Enos 1:3) to "and my soul hungered" (Enos 1:4). The leap requires plowing through intervening material about the words of Enos's father and then intuiting perceptive symbolic connections that are veiled and disconnected.

2. Wrestling and Appearing "Before"

When Enos says he is going to "tell you of the wrestle which [he] had before God," he is again speaking symbolically. Yet he does not clarify that wrestling is symbolic, nor does he point out what that symbolism could mean, which leaves both decisions up to the reader. Furthermore, the sentence about wrestling complicates the narrative with an unclear audience. Enos is obviously going to tell a story, but to whom? He may be speaking to an inside-the-text audience, an idea supported by his concluding "Amen" and his occasional use of first-person plural pronouns, such as "*our* strugglings" against the Lamanites who wanted to "destroy *our* records and *us*" (Enos 1:14, my emphasis). But Enos also uses first person singular pronouns, referring to "my brethren, the Nephites" (Enos 1:9) or "my people, the Nephites" (Enos 1:13). He uses this pronoun style more often than the inclusive plural pronouns, thus indicating that he is speaking *of* the Nephites, not *to* the Nephites.

Whomever Enos thinks he is his audience, he is planning to tell them about his wrestle before God. Many things are done "before God" in the Book of Mormon. Of the possible actions, it is most common to humble oneself *before God*, to stand *before God* (on judgment day), or to walk *before God* in a variety of manners, such as "uprightly" or "blamelessly." Only one other person wrestles in the Book of Mormon: Alma₂, and Alma₂ does not wrestle *before* God; he wrestles *with* God. Despite a few substantial differences, both Alma₂ and Enos name this wrestling as "mighty prayer" (Enos 1:4; Alma 8:10), leading readers to believe that Enos's purpose is to tell a story of fervent prayer addressed to God and also *before* God but not *with* God.

Comparatively, Psalm 42/43 has a more definite audience and also a more thorough explication of "before God." While many psalms do not have contextual information, Psalm 42/43 has a superscription: it is explicitly addressed to the "Chief Musician, Maschil, for the sons of Korah."[11] Korah lead a rebellion against Moses in Numbers 16, and, as punishment, "the earth opened her mouth, and swallowed them

---

11. See superscription to Psalm 42 in KJV. Some other versions of the Bible include the dedicatory information into verse 1.

[Korah and his followers] up, and their houses, and all the men that *appertained* unto Korah, and all *their* goods" (Numbers 16:30). Nevertheless, the sons of Korah re-established themselves as "'gatekeepers' in the temple (1 Chron 26:1, 19) and temple singers (2 Chron 20:19)."[12] Like Enos, the psalmist's desire is to be "before the Lord" (Ps 42:2). The Hebrew word translated as "before" or "in front of" in Psalm 42:2 technically means "face" but can also be translated as "presence" or "in the presence of" to "face" or "person."[13] Thus other translations of Psalm 42:2 range from the New International Version's (NIV) "When can I go and meet with God?" to the New American Standard Bible's (NASB) "When shall I come and appear before God?" to the more literally translated "When shall I come and behold the face of God?" (Amplified Bible).

Enos's initial statement of purpose (to tell the story of his wrestle before God) and the psalmist's stated purpose (appearing before the Lord) are similar, and both writers move toward effective closure by circling back around to these purposes in their conclusions. The psalmist circles back around with straightforward statements; the psalmist desires God to "send out thy light and thy truth" so that those traits can "lead me . . . unto thy holy hill and to thy tabernacles" (Psalm 43:3), even right to the "altar of God" (Psalm 43:4). The psalmist's initial desire to appear before God could have been understood in a post-mortal sense, but the third stanza clarifies that this is a present-day desire with statements about the temple, calling it a holy hill, tabernacles, and the altar of God. As Jiri Moskala summarizes: "To appear before God's face points to visiting the sanctuary . . . [and] to see God's face

---

12. Walker-Jones, Arthur. *Psalms Book 2*, 26. Their role in the temple explains why they would be collecting of a group of "Korah" psalms, namely Psalms 42–49, 84–85, and 87–88. In her commentary on *Psalms Book 2-3*, Denise Dombkowski Hopkins quotes John Vassar's assessment, "Korah may function as 'the archtype of rebellion,' but his descendants become 'the archetype of restitution and return." See Hopkins, *Wisdom Commentary*, 5.

13. James Strong, "6440. pə-nê," *The New Strong's Expanded Exhaustive Concordance of the Bible, Red-Letter Edition* (Nashville, Tenn: Thomas Nelson, 2001), 228–229

was an expression for worshipping God in the Temple."[14] The psalmist's straightforward desire is to "come and appear before God," meaning to go to the holy sanctuary (Psalm 42:2).

Enos concludes with a projection of a post-mortal image of himself. He envisions the moment when he will "stand *before*" his Redeemer (Enos 1:27, my emphasis), wording that lightly echoes his initial wish to tell of "the wrestle which [he] had *before* God" (Enos 1:1). The echo is weaker than the strong, unmistakable temple imagery in Psalm 42/43, which explicitly connects temple worship, being *before God*, and seeing his face. Nevertheless, the Book of Mormon has a similar understanding of *before God*. For example, in Alma 15:17, people "humble themselves *before God*, and [begin] to assemble themselves together at their sanctuaries to worship God *before the altar*" (my emphasis). If Enos's wrestle *before God* can be understood in the biblical sense, his conclusion is strengthened. In one of the only uses of visual imagery, Enos announces that in the afterlife, he will "stand before" his Redeemer and "see his *face* with pleasure" (Enos 1:27, my emphasis).

If Enos is speaking literally, then he is hunting and wrestling in a forest. If he is speaking symbolically, then importing the context of temple worship from the Psalm to Enos's narrative makes sense. It is supported by Sharon Harris's work. She also finds that "the references in Psalms [132] and . . . 'the joy of the saints' connects to covenants and temple worship" in Enos's story.[15] The third stanza of Psalm 42/43 expands, restates, and clarifies the psalmist's original request to appear before God, making it abundantly clear that the psalmist desires temple worship. Enos, contrastingly, wrestles before God and plans to stand before God after this life. A viable interpretation of those statements is temple worship, though whether that meaningful context was intended is unclear.

---

14. Jiri Moskala, "The Indispensable God's Presence: Toward the Theology of God's Face." *Faculty Publications,* (2020), 2411. https://digitalcommons.andrews.edu/pubs/2411. See also John Goldingay. *Psalms : Volume 2 (Baker Commentary on the Old Testament Wisdom and Psalms): Psalms 42–89.* (Ada, Michigan: Baker Publishing Group, 2007).

15. Sharon Harris, *Enos, Jarom, Omni: A Brief Theological Introduction.* (Provo, UT: Neal A. Maxwell Institute for Religious Scholarship, 2020), 25.

3. All Day and Night

Perhaps his lack of clarity is why Enos needs to cry such a lengthy prayer. Enos cries "all the day long . . . and when the night came, [he] did still raise [his] voice high" (Enos 1:4). This dramatic description evokes a lengthy duration of time without suggesting frequency. In other words, it seems most likely that Enos's prayer is an hours-long, one-off event. His words are another point of connection with Psalm 42/43, since the psalmist weeps "day and night."[16] Weeping and prayer are technically different, though in this circumstance, they likely mean the same thing. Psalm 42/43 is typically classified as an "individual lament,"[17] a psalm or song that is in essence an evocative prayer of sorrow written (or spoken or sung) as a "legitimate complaint in faith to God."[18] In other words, the Psalm is a prayer, correlating with Enos's prayer narrative. If the psalmist's tears are not prayer but cries, this point of connection still exists. Enos twice describes his prayer as a "cry" (Enos 1:4). Even when he "raises [his] voice high," he may well be weeping. In *The Sense of Scripture: Sensory Perception in the Hebrew Bible*, Yael Avrahami notes that the Hebrew verb meaning "to lift" appears 17 times with voice in the Hebrew Bible, regularly combining into "audio imagery" and forming a "phrase [that] describes weeping."[19] Tears before the Lord and prayers to the Lord are similar in this situation: both are cried.

Despite the paralleled prayer/cry and day/night connections, Psalm 42/43 describes multiple prayers. In the first stanza, the psalmist states that "tears have been my meat day and night," connoting ongoing prayer. The psalmist underscores the day and night imagery in the second stanza, recognizing that the Lord "command[s] his lovingkindness

---

16. Sharon Harris also points out that approximately one-third of the day and night echoes in scripture are found in various psalms. See Harris, *Enos, Jarom, Omni*, 24.

17. Hopkins, *Wisdom Commentary*, 6.

18. Densise Dombkowski Hopkins, *Journey through the Psalms* (St. Louis, MO. Chalice Press, 2002), 81.

19. Yael Avrahami, *The Senses of Scripture: Sensory Perception in the Hebrew Bible*, Library of Hebrew Bible/Old Testament Series, edited by Claudia V. Camp and Andrew Mein, (NY: Bloomsbury, 2014), 81.

in the daytime, and in the night his song shall be with me" (Psalm 42:8). With this repetition, the psalmist effectively marks a past of searching for God and a present of continued searching. The psalmist prays to "the God of my life" (Psalm 42:8), a loving name-title that also indicates ongoing prayer to the God of life for the duration of life.

The day and night practice of regular prayer is further supported by the structure of Psalm 42/43. A shared refrain occurs at the conclusion of each stanza. In each refrain, the psalmist seemingly speaks to self, telling his or her own soul to "hope thou in God, for I shall yet praise him" (Psalm 42:5, 11; Psalm 43:5). After the third iteration of this promise to praise God yet again, readers assume that this psalmist intends to pray tonight, tomorrow morning, and every day. The repetitious refrain punctuates the psalmist's lament almost as night and day punctuate every twenty-four hours or as regular prayer punctuates a saint's life.

Comparatively, Enos's long prayer may conclude in verse 8 with Enos being told, "thy faith hath made thee whole" (Enos 1:8) or it may conclude in verse 10 when Enos is told, "I will visit thy brethren according as I have said" (Enos 1:10). Enos initially prays until he hears a "voice" say, "thy sins are forgiven thee, and thou shalt be blessed" (Enos 1:5), but this is not the end of his prayer. Enos continues the discussion by asking, "Lord, how is it done" (Enos 1:7). The Lord responds with a lengthy answer in verse 8. The next verse explains that "when" Enos heard the Lord's words, he "began to feel a desire for the welfare of my brethren" (Enos 1:9), and that desire provokes Enos to further prayer, this time described as Enos "pour[ing] out [his] whole soul unto God" for his Nephite brethren. Is this "pouring" included in the day and night of Enos's one long prayer—or is it a new prayer? That depends on the amount of time that passes between the first small feelings of "a desire for the welfare" of others and a feeling of overwhelming love that inspires one to "pour out [one's] whole soul unto God" for others (Enos 1:9). While that feeling may blossom quickly, it also could take years to move from intimations of empathy to a state of responsive (and responsible) pouring out of one's soul.

In yet another point of connection, the psalmist also pours out soul, stating, "When I remember these things, I pour out my soul in me." Both Enos and the psalmist "pour out" themselves, a process called kenosis. Harris defines kenosis as "self-emptying," or a process of pouring out of one's own power or self with "focused, complete commitment to the life and welfare of specific people."[20] Both Enos and the psalmist enact this process because of others' actions, but for very different reasons. Enos pours out his soul unto God for his Nephite brothers because of his concern for their welfare.

The psalmist remembers his or her own tears and being mocked with words such as, "Where is thy God?" (Psalm 42:3). It isw the tears and mocking that causes the psalmist to self-empty (Psalm 42:4). The psalmist states, "when I remember these things, I pour out my soul in me: for I had gone with the multitude to the house of God, with the voice of joy and praise, with the multitude that kept holyday" (Psalm 42:4). Most scholars assume that the psalmist invokes a memory of a holy festival at the temple to counteract his or her present sad situation. And yet the phrasing seems to suggest that something the psalmist found at the house of God is connected to pain and tears instead of rejoicing. Nevertheless, the psalmist repeats the refrain, promising hope in God and more tears and prayers tomorrow.

Enos's all-day-and-into-the-night prayer is a prayer of endurance, but how many times he prayed and how long he prayed is trapped in the convoluted chronology of his story. His reliance on sequencing in this story is absolutely necessary given that indecipherable chronology, hidden duration, and unclear frequency. In comparison, Psalm 42/43 has clear content, repeated day/night imagery that connotes frequency and chronology, as well as a thrice-repeated refrain that is structurally so powerful that there is no other way to understand it.[21]

4. Hunger and Thirst

Despite Enos's ambiguity, his statement, "my soul hungered" (Enos 1:4), obviously parallels the poet's statement, "my soul thirsts" (Psalm 42:2). The phrasings are similar both syntactically (pronoun, noun, verb) and

---

20. Harris, *Enos, Jarom, Omni*, 30.

21. Paul R. Raabe. *Psalm Structures: A Study of Psalms with Refrains.* (United Kingdom: Bloomsbury Publishing, 1990), 44.

the subject is lexically identical ("my soul"). The actions of hungering and thirsting are different but equal, complementary life-sustaining actions, required necessities for a physical body to survive. Surprisingly few *souls* hunger in scripture[22] and even fewer *souls* thirst.[23] More souls *hunger and thirst*[24], though none do in the Book of Mormon after Jesus declares in 3 Nephi 20:8 that the "soul" of those who partake of the sacrament "shall never hunger nor thirst, but shall be filled." The *Dictionary of Biblical Imagery* explains that the two "physical sensations . . . are linked repeatedly with the felt need for spiritual resources, goodness or communion with God himself." The motif should remind readers that "humanity lives in daily, hourly dependence—both physical and spiritual—on God."[25]

Despite being complementary halves, the psalmist does not need Enos's hunger to be whole. The psalmist thirsts for God and a mere verse later evokes food imagery by describing "tears" that are his or her "meat" (3). These words effectively double the desire for God by stating it in terms of thirst and hunger—and then double that desire again with phrasing that includes inherent physical and spiritual need. The poet is thirsting and hungering for God through physical language with clear spiritual implications. The need for God is whole, mature, and encompassing.

Enos's desire is stated in terms of hunger alone. He has only one-half of the physical necessities of life, leaving him incomplete and unbalanced. But Enos's hunger not only lacks accompanying thirst, it is even less than a complete complementary half: the hunger itself is incomplete. In a glaring silence, Enos declares in Enos 1:4, "And my soul

---

22. Only 3 verses in the Book of Mormon one of which is a quotation from Isaiah speak of souls that hunger: 2 Ne 27:3, Enos 1:4, and 3 Nephi 20:8; only 3 books in the Old Testament speak of hungry souls that combine to total of 8 Old Testament verses: Psalms 107:5, 9; Proverbs 6:30, 19:15, 27:7; and Isaiah 29:8, 32:6; 58:10.

23. Only 2 verses in the Book of Mormon, one of which is a quotation from Isaiah, speak of souls that thirst: 2 Ne 27:3, and 3 Ne 20:8

24. The pairing of hungering and thirsting in the Book of Mormon often appears as a triplet: hunger, thirst, and fatigue.

25. Leland Ryken, James C. Wilhoit, and Tremper Longman III. "Appetite." *Dictionary of Biblica Imagery* (Downers Grove, Ill.: IVP Academic, 1998), 40.

hungered . . ." Enos's hunger is not merely less; it is completely unde-
fined. He does not offer a vague answer; he offers no answer. He simply
hungers. The statement conveys real need or desire. But for what? And
is he not thirsty as well? King Benjamin is the only other person in the
Book of Mormon who speaks of someone's "own soul." Three times
during his sermon, King Benjamin refers to a person's "own soul"—and
each one of those instances is about people who "drink damnation"
to their souls (see Mosiah 2:33; 3:18; 25). Without more explanation,
readers flounder and wonder: did Enos hunger for unhealthy spiritual
food or have a thirst that would bring about damnation? Comparing
Enos with Psalm 42/43 again highlights the gaps in Enos's story: he
relies on only one-half of a complementary process—and he does so in
an open-ended and indiscriminate manner, never specifying exactly
what his soul hungers for.

Though the psalmist and Enos state that it is their "souls" that hunger or thirst, it is unlikely that the psalmist would state that dependence
on God as "physical and spiritual" need, as if the self were partitioned.
The word translated as "soul" in Psalm 42:1 can simply be referring to
"oneself" or a "living being," but modern readers are likely thinking
of *soul* as a spirit within a body. Robert Di Vito argues that the sense
that one is what one thinks, that the life-giving site of individuality
can be separated from the physical self/body is foreign to ancient Israelite culture. There is no dichotomy, no separation between "soul and
body in the manner of Greek dualism." Instead of separation, a person was a "totality."[26] Thus for the psalmist to say, "my soul thirsteth
for God" and then ask "when shall I come and appear before God"
is not pitting some inner desire for God against a sluggish physical
self. Instead, both lines are saying the same thing. The psalmist is not
expressing "hidden depths" of personhood and then commenting on
a plan for external action that may or may not be stronger or weaker
than, or even simply different than intent or desire.[27] As Robert Di
Vito explains in his widely cited article, "Old Testament Anthropology

---

26. Robert A. Di Vito, "Old Testament Anthropology and the Construction of Personal Identity," *The Catholic Biblical Quarterly* 61, no. 2 (1999), 226.

27. Di Vito, "Old Testament Anthropology," 232.

and the Construction of Personal Identity," what a person manifests externally is who that person is; the "lack of inner depths means people 'reveal' themselves through their concrete behavior."[28]

If this idea of Israelite self is transferable to Enos, then Enos may not be as silent as he seems. Though there is no direct object targeted by his hunger, the actions that follow may be inseparable from his desires. Enos hungered—and then he "kneeled down before [his] Maker, and cried unto him in mighty prayer and supplication for [his] own soul" (Enos 1:4). That action is the desire of his soul, if his soul is like the soul of an Israelite psalmist. For Enos to "hunger" may be the same as what he then expresses through physical action. As Di Vito points out, there is a single Hebrew word that is translated as "both 'hearing' and 'obeying' in the OT" and another word that "is used for both 'knowing' and 'choosing.'"[29] In his own narrative and through his own words, Enos's desires and actions are disconnected. His soul does one thing, and his body does another. However, to the degree that Enos's sense of self is similar to personal identity in the Hebrew Bible, he is not as separated from his soul as it may seem.

5. Implications

If actions define someone, the psalmist and Enos may be quite similar. Their initial actions and experiences are parallel, albeit re-ordered. The psalmist thirsts (Psalm 42:2) and Enos hungers (Enos 1:4). The psalmist cries "tears . . . day and night" to God (Psalm 42:3), and Enos "crie[s] unto [his Maker] in mighty prayer . . . all the day long" and is still praying "when the night came" (Enos 1:4, my emphasis). The psalmist is longing to "appear *before God*" at least in part because of the memory of the "*voice of joy* and praise" that attends those saintly people who enter "the "house of God" (Psalms 42:4, my emphasis) and Enos, similarly, "wrestles *before God*" (Enos 1:2, my emphasis) and remembers his "father *speak[ing]*" the words "concerning eternal life, and the *joy* of the saints" (Enos 1:4, my emphasis). The psalmist says, "*I pour out*

---

28. Di Vito, "Old Testament Anthropology," 233.
29. Di Vito, "Old Testament Anthropology," 230.

my soul in me" (Psalms 42:4, my emphasis).[30] Despite reordered actions and intervening actions, Enos says, "*I did pour out my whole soul*" (Enos 1:9, my emphasis). The echoes between the texts are substantial (though not lengthy), surprisingly parallel, and centered in the same area of both texts.

What readers notice is that Enos may not be who they thought he was. He seems strangely well-defined by eight words, "I went to hunt beasts in the forest"—and yet that independent clause is just that: independent. Unlike the actions of the psalmist, Enos's actions are not connected. The first eight verses are filled with verbs that tell of action, but those actions are initially both cause-less and un-causing. They are correlated by proximity, but they are not dependent upon each other. Enos went to hunt, but that hunt does not trigger the words of his father to come to his mind. The words seem to do that of their own volition. Neither those words nor the memory of them produces a hunger in his soul. His soul simply hungers. When he cries unto his Maker in mighty prayer, it is not because his soul hungered. He soul just hungers. Then he cries. Each action is an island—sometimes connected by "and" but not connected in any meaningful sense by causality. Enos's "story" has no plot—at least, not in the first eight verses. This plot-less narrative is not a story but a list of actions without motives. If he states feelings at all, they do not create any discernible effect. Any supposition about Enos's intent for hunting or crying or telling his story, and any speculation about the effects of his hunger or his knowledge of his father or the impacts of his actions is simply supposition.

What is holding Enos's story together if it not connected by cause and effect? It is not Enos's relationships. Enos is not connected to his brethren, the Nephites, or his brethren, the Lamanites, until after he is "made whole" (Enos 1:8). Indeed, he has such disconnection with those around him that he seemingly has no concern for others until he is made whole. This disconnection may be tied to Enos's method of

---

30. Referring to Psalm 42:7 (which uses the same wording as verse 4), Di Vito points out the "the preposition is used here to indicate the oppressive force or weight of the 'soul,' not within the person but, from the Hebrew point of view, upon the victim who is suffering, as if from the outside." See Di Vito, "Old Testament Anthropology," 229.

experiencing the world. If Enos engages with his environment mainly through sound and aural/oral means, he is likely comprehending his world by sound, according to Nicole Tilford. Unlike people who privilege the sight/visual modality (with its spatial orientation), hearing is a time-focused, "sequential" modality.[31] Sounds can occur at the same time, but they all occur over a duration of time, even if it is a very short duration.[32] Notably, this sequencing is what Enos's narrative reflects: actions that occur "before" (Enos 1:2) or "while" (Enos 1:10) or "after" (Enos 1:11) other actions. The sequencing orders actions in time; it lines them up, but it does so without indicating how long each takes to occur.

This matters because time matters to Enos. Modern readers classify his prayers by what or by whom he prays for but differentiating Enos's prayer by content is challenging. Modern readers regularly and somewhat simplistically say this is a narrative of three prayers: prayer for self, friends (own people), and enemies (others).[33] The first two descriptions are adequate, though readers cannot be certain since content is not recorded. Enos describes his prayer for the Nephites by announcing that he "did pour out [his] whole soul for them" (Enos 1:9). Perhaps he prayed "for" the Nephites by requesting some outlandish thing, and God's answer in verse 10 is a "no" in the form of a restatement of the positive aspect of the Lehite covenant. The same problem exists for Enos's prayer for his own soul, though the specificity of "a voice" saying, "Thy sins are forgiven thee" makes it likely that Enos's "mighty prayer and supplication for [his] own soul" focused specifically on the state of his soul.

---

31. Nicole L. Tilford. *Sensing World, Sensing Wisdom: The Cognitive Foundation of Biblical Metaphors. Ancient Israel and Its Literature.* (Atlanta, GA: SBL Press, 2017), 69–74.

32. Tilford. *Sensing World, Sensing Wisdom,* 69–74.

33. The student manual for college-aged institute students reads: "After feeling the blessings of the Atonement for himself, Enos prayer for the welfare of his own people, the Nephites, and then for the spiritual welfare of his enemies, the Lamanites." See "Enos 1:9–15. A Desire for the Welfare of Others," in "Chapter 17: Enos-Words of Mormon," *Book of Mormon Student Manual: Religion 121–122,* (SLC, UT: The Church of Jesus Christ of Latter-day Saints), 131.

In any case, describing verse 13 as a prayer "for the Lamanites" seems inaccurate, regardless of whether Enos thinks he "prayed . . . for [his] brethren, the Lamanites" (Enos 1:11). The prayer in verse 13 reiterates only the negative (punishing) aspect of the Lehite covenant. As such, it is inherently a prayer *against* the Lamanites. Their self-determined desire as stated by Enos is to "destroy" the Nephites, their records, and their traditions (Enos 1:14). Inasmuch as verse 13 is a prayer that "'God [will] preserve a record of my people, the Nephites," it is a prayer that opposes Lamanite self-determination (presumably judging it as sinful) while simultaneously asking that the Nephites be blessed with their desire (preserved records), despite the Nephite nation sinning unto destruction. Enos's prayer "for my brethren, the Lamanites" is only a prayer "for" the Lamanites in the loosest sense of the term—and, even then, is more of a prayer for Lamanite descendants living thousands of years in the future.

The third stanza of Psalm 42/43 is also focused on the future, and it is part of the strong 3-part structure of Psalm 42/43. Many scholars see this as a past-present-future structure within the genre of a lament.[34] The repetition of the refrain is so forceful that any other structure is simply not persuasive. The possibility of similar structure should be considered in light of Enos's commitment to sequencing despite jumbled chronology, and verb tense changes. These changeable verbs challenge precise chronology. For example, in verse 10, Enos explains part of his prayer and God's answer about his Nephite brethren [line breaks created to emphasize verbs]:

> Enos "was thus struggling in the spirit [past progressive verb],"
> when "the voice of the Lord came into his mind again [simple past],
> saying [continuous present],
> I will visit [simple future]
> thy brethren as I have said [present perfect]."

---

34. See, for example, Luis Alonso Schökel. "The Poetic Structure of Psalm 42–43." *Journal for the Study of the Old Testament* 1, no. 1 (1976): 4–11.

> After Enos "had heard [past perfect]
> these words" spoken by the Lord, his "faith began to be
> unshaken" [inceptive verb/infinitive] (Enos 1:11).

The verbs move from past to the continuous present to promises for the future stated in the past and lasting to the present in ways that began impacting him at a set moment in time.

As if the verb tense shifts were not enough, Enos states plainly in verse 14 that "at the present" his strugglings for the Lamanites "were vain" [past tense] (Enos 1:14). Presumably, when Enos says "at the present," he is referring to his present, namely the moment in which he is writing retrospectively about events in his past. But then the story continues moving forward to prayers and action that are in the future rather than the "present" of Enos's present. Verse 15, for example, states that Enos "cried unto [the Lord] continually" about the records and their preservation. He does so because the Lord "had said [past perfect] unto [him]: whatsoever thing ye shall ask in faith in the name of Christ, ye shall receive it" (Enos 1:15). This prayer is stated as if it were Enos's response in the past to God's answer to Enos's prayer offered even further in the past. Indeed, it is in effect the same answer as verse 12, but stated more generally and solely in terms of faith rather than desire. That makes sense because verse 12 is the answer to Enos's summarized prayer in verse 13. The answer as stated in verse 12 is that the Lord will grant Enos's desires because of his faith. Bizarrely, that makes verse 15 and 16 the third time that Enos sums up his convoluted "third" prayer for the Lamanites and the records [see chart: Prayer 3: Prayer for the Future (Lamanites and Records)]. In essence, Enos re-states his "many long strugglings" prayer and answer in verses 11–12, 13, and 15 and 16, which makes his comment about Nephite-Lamanite relations "at the present" a bizarre comment that is not in Enos's "present" lived moment, but in a "present" moment that is merely in the middle of Enos's past.

This story is told by Enos and set some time in Enos's murky past, his murkier present, and occasionally in his future, which is also the reader's present. The whole thing is strangely adrift in time, somewhat atemporal despite sequencing. Comparison with Psalm 42/43 suggests the possibility that Enos's prayers are exactly for whom he says they are for (self, Nephites, and Lamanites), but they are less about audience and more about an effort to match the past-present-future temporality that Psalm 42/43 displays. If so, then the issue at stake is less about what or whom he prays for and more about the temporal setting of whom or what he prays for. He prays for the Lamanites of the future, and he prays for his Nephite brothers in the present, but *when*—what "time"? what setting?—is Enos's prayer for his own soul?

6. Further Implications

Despite the words of gratitude for his father, Enos is disconnected. Overlaying his narrative with Psalm 42/43 pulls these disconnections to the surface. He wrestles, but only *before* God, not *with* God. Readers do not know whether the wrestle *before God* refers to a literal or symbolic setting or both. Wherever the wrestle is, it is done all day and into the night. That timing is clear, though what happens during that timing is not clear at all, nor is it obvious why what happens during that one long wrestling happens. Presumably things happen because Enos hungers for them to happen, but his initial actions are disconnected and he never specifies for what he is hungering. He may be hungering for the remission of his sins, for the welfare of his all of his brethren, or the welfare for some of his brethren and for the records of his fathers. Then again, he may simply be hungering for the beasts he is hunting.

That becomes extraordinarily troubling when read through the overlay of Psalm 42/43. The psalmist's connection to the deer in Psalm 42/43 is clearly implied in the first stanza. Both are thirsty and searching, paralleling each other in need and action. Symbolically, the deer with its third person feminine singular actions is the voice of the psalmist. Enos is not the beasts. He is a hunter of beasts. Though Nephi slays wild beasts in the tops of the mountains after the broken bow incident, Nephi's narrative is a literal story about hunger and food and the real possibility of starvation. Enos's story may not be as obviously symbolic as Psalm 42/43, but it is also not as obviously literal as Nephi's.

The very word that causes readers to think they know Enos is the problem: hunt. Hunting is deeply problematic in the Book of Mormon. Hunt is used twelve times in this book of scripture. Enos hunts beasts, and in the book of Ether, Lib and his people also "hunt food for the people of the land" (Ether 10:19). Like Enos, they hunt in a land that is "covered with animals of the forest" (Ether 10:19). In a strange coincidence that evokes the ancient myths about deer, the same verse that tells of Lib and his hunting mentions that "the poisonous serpents were destroyed" in the days of Lib (Ether 10:19).

Enos's hunt and Lib's hunt are the outside edges; they frame the use of "hunt" in the Book of Mormon. The ten other uses of hunt all refer to the hunting of people. Dismissing Lib's hunt because of the exceptionality of the Book of Ether leaves Enos as the lone hunter of "beasts." Notably, Nephi slays beasts, but he does not *hunt* them, and considering the overwhelming use of hunt in conjunction with people, it is suddenly necessary to know what verb describes Nephi's actions. Hunting overwhelming describes searching for or pursuing people, so it matters that Nephi did not hunt beasts.

What is Enos doing when he hunts for beasts? The words about animals and hunting, beasts and deer, women and actions, and weeping and prayers, cluster around Enos in a disturbing tornado. What are "beasts"? Why is Enos hunting them? Why is it clearly a derogatory statement to say that Lamanites eat raw "beasts of prey" (Enos 1:20)? Nephi is the only other person in the Book of Mormon who speaks of "beasts of prey," and he moves straight from saying that the Lamanites "seek in the wilderness" for them (2 Ne 5:24) to the negative side of the Lehite covenant, noting that the Lamanites "shall scourge [the Nephites] even unto destruction" if the Nephites will not remember their God (2 Ne 5:25). Numbers 31:11 is the only place with similar phrasing, and it comfortingly delineates "beasts of prey" as the "beeves" and "sheep" and "asses" which were collected as "booty" after war with the Midianites (Num 31:30–32). But the booty also included "prey of men," a horrific phrase that refers to thousands of Midianite women and children taken in the war.

Without more specificity, more straightforward statements, and perfectly crystalline examples, this cluster of words and their disturbing innuendos should be discounted or rejected. And yet, Enos does hunt beasts. Using those words only as the lightest of suggestions about the quality of an interaction (negative) and the object of an interaction (women), and, moreover, using the overlay of Psalm 42/43 as a hint about directionality in time (past) means looking to Enos's past for a problem with women. Following the vague suggestion connects Enos to his father Jacob's sermon at the temple. What seems uncertain and highly speculative lands readers in a steady stream of word echoes and so many points of connection that it seems strange not to have recognized these connections before. Whether Enos heard Jacob's vigorous chastisement of Nephite men for their mistreatment of their wives and children firsthand or truly "heard" it as an adult in written form, it seems entirely possible that Enos was like other Nephite men, beginning to sin by "hunting" for new wives and concubines, and justifying his sexual "crimes" (Jacob 2:23)

Jacob speaks from "the temple" and he does so to "declare unto you the word of God" (Jacob 2:2). Enos speaks of his wrestle "before God" (Enos 1:2), which is at least an oblique reference to working before God's eyes and possibly a straight up reference to the temple. Jacob is working under a "strict commandment which [he has] received from God to *admonish*" the Nephite men (Jacob 2:9, my emphasis), and Enos praises his father for teaching him the "*admonition* of the Lord" (Enos 1:1, my emphasis). Enos is particular: he is grateful specifically for the "admonition *of the Lord*," which connects his gratitude to Jacob's teachings at the temple, specifically those about women: in a short but powerful ten verses (Jacob 2:23–33), Jacob refers fourteen different times *to the Lord* in various phrases such as "thus saith the Lord" (Jacob 2:23, 25, 28) or the slightly shorter "saith the Lord" [Jacob 2:24, 29, 30, 32 (twice), 33].[35] Enos is also grateful to his father for teaching him in the "nurture . . . of the Lord" (Enos 1:1). The only other use of "nuture" in all of scripture is in Ephesians 6:4, in which the Greek word for nurture refers to the things which "[cultivate] the soul, especially by correcting mistakes and curbing the passions; hence, instruction which aims at the increase of virtue."[36]

---

35. Becca Driggs, a former student, informed me of this insight.

36. "3809. Paideia," Bible Hub, Thayer's Greek Lexicon, https://biblehub.com/text/ephesians/6-4.htm.

In a series of connections, Enos praises his father for teaching him the words "concerning eternal life and the *joy* of the saints" (Enos 1:3, my emphasis). Jacob finishes his sermon at the temple and speaks of the "few words" he has written, hoping that his "children" and his "beloved brethren" (Enos 4:2) will "learn with *joy*" about their "first parents" (Enos 4:3). After praying for his "own soul," Enos prays for the "welfare of his brethren," possibly having heard Jacob's great "anxiety for the welfare of your souls" (Jacob 2:3). Jacob labors "diligently . . . [to] persuade [the people] to come unto Christ . . . that they might enter into his rest" (Jacob 1:7), and Enos refers three different times to that "rest" in his short one-chapter book.[37] Jacob reminds the men that they already "know" these commandments, and that that knowledge creates consequences. Jacob frames this idea as a statement of knowledge linked to a consequence, stating that because they know things, "wherefore . . . ye have come unto great condemnation; for ye have done these things which ye ought not to have done" (Jacob 2:34). Enos uses the same construction of "knowing" connected to a "wherefore" statement four times in his prayer narrative (see Enos 1:6, 9, 15, 17). Besides these words from the temple sermon, Enos also connects with Jacob in other sermons, though less frequently than the temple sermon.[38]

---

37. See Enos 1:17, 27 (two uses).

38. When Enos asks, "Lord, how is it done?" (Enos 1:7), the Lord's answer is a reminder of Christ, who shall "manifest himself in the flesh" and a commandment to act, "Wherefore, go to" (Enos 1:8). There are only five verses in scripture that discuss Christ "manifesting himself in the flesh." Three of the five are in Nephi's writings. In all three statements, Nephi adds a prepositional phrase in the middle, specifying who Christ is manifesting himself "unto." The other two uses of that phrase are both uninterrupted; Jacob speaks directly of Christ, urging his "beloved brethren" to seek for "a hope of glory in him before he manifesteth himself in the flesh" (Jacob 4:11). Enos speaks of Christ, saying that he will "see his face with pleasure" (Enos 1:27), even though "many years pass away before [the Savior] will manifest himself in the flesh" (Enos 1:8). When the Lord tells Enos, "Wherefore, go to," he is urging action in phraseology used only three times in scripture: this use in Enos 1:8, one use by Jacob in the allegory of the olive tree (Jacob 5:61) and (D&C 54:7). Also linking father and son exclusively is the phrase "labored with all diligence." Jacob uses the phrase in his allegory of the olive tree, and Enos uses it when he explains his long struggling prayer for the Lamanites and records (see Jacob 5:74 and Enos 1:12). After Enos prays for the Nephites, the Lord tells him, "their transgressions will I bring down with sorrow upon their own heads" (Enos 1:10).

In a critical word-level link between father and son, Jacob explains that he is personally devastated by these men's actions. He says their behavior causes him to "shrink with shame before the presence of *my Maker*" (Jacob 2:6, my emphasis). In his narrative of hunting beasts and repentance, Enos says, "I kneeled down before *my Maker*, and I cried unto him in mighty prayer and supplication for mine own soul" (Enos 1:4, my emphasis). Jacob uses the title "my Maker" just once. Enos uses the title "my Maker" just once. No one else in the Book of Mormon refers to God as their own personal "Maker."[39]

Jacob's nurture and admonition of the Lord brings Enos to a remission of sins. Jacob is the first to preach of "guilt" in the Book of Mormon, reminding his people that a "glorious day of justice" is coming (2 Ne 9:46). All of us "shall have a perfect knowledge of all our guilt" (2 Ne 9:14). Those who have not repented will find that the "happiness which is prepared for the saints" is hid from them forever (2 Ne 9:43). If they do not repent, they will "be constrained to exclaim: . . . I know my guilt" (2 Ne 9:46). What they must do to avoid this guilt is "pray unto him continually by day and give thanks unto his holy name by night" (2 Ne 9:52). Though these teachings are not from Jacob's temple sermon, they tell someone how to repent and why. Enos seems to be responding directly to his father's teachings. He tells of his "wrestle . . . before God" and the "words" his father spoke about the "joy of the saints" (Enos 1:2, 3). He prays "all the day long" and kept praying "when the night came" (Enos 1:4). Receiving a remission of sins, Enos declares, "My guilt was swept away" (Enos 1:6). So many people repent in scripture, but no one

---

This is a different understanding than Jacob's willingness to take "upon [himself] the responsibility" of "answering the sins of the people on our own heads if we did not teach them" (Jacob 1:19). That may come to Enos in time, since he does receive the gospel so fully that he "went about among the people of Nephi" to teach them (Enos 1:19), although he does not seem to have the same role and responsibility that Jacob had.

39. Nephi speaks of "thy Maker" (2 Ne 8:13) and "your Maker" (2 Ne 9:40). In Helaman 1:11, the Gadianton robbers swear by "their everlasting Maker," and in 3 Ne 22:5, Jesus quotes Isaiah 54, stating, "For thy maker, thy husband, the Lord of Hosts is his name." Job speaks of "my Maker" three times, making him the only person besides Jacob and Enos to do so (see Job 32:22, 35:10, 36:3).

else owns their personal guilt like Enos.[40] Enos claims his guilt, having learned to say "my guilt" from the only other person in scripture who speaks of guilt in the first person, singular: his father, Jacob. Repenting does not turn Enos from his father, but, rather, pulls him closer. Enos says his "faith began to be unshaken" (Enos 1:11). Nephi speaks of "unshaken faith" in 2 Ne 31:19, but he does so without qualifications or reservations. Jacob, however, teaches that "our faith becometh unshaken" (Jacob 4:6), phrasing that Enos imitates. No one else in scripture speaks of "unshaken faith," much less the beginning or ending of it.

Perhaps readers should have expected Enos and Jacob to use similar words. And yet, it is unlikely that any modern readers expect Jacob's words to the Nephite women to resonate with the words of Psalm 42/43 and the psalmist's desperate thirst for hope from the living God. Jacob is deeply concerned about the need to admonish the men because he fears that the women who have come to the temple to "hear the pleasing word of God" will instead hear words that will "enlarge the wounds of those who are already wounded" (Jacob 2:9). Jacob has reason to be anxious: he fears the "strictness of the word of God" will cause "many hearts [to die]" (Jacob 2:38). The psalmist recalls going with the "multitude" to the "house of God" on the "holyday," hoping to hear words spoken by "the voice of joy and rejoicing" (Psalm 42:4). Jacob is anxious that his words for the men will be like "daggers placed to pierce [the women's] souls and wound their delicate minds" (Jacob 2:9). There are no other "daggers" in scripture, yet the speaker of Psalm 42/43 cries to the Lord that "mine enemies reproach me" and it feels like a "sword in my bones" when "they say daily unto me, 'Where is thy God?'" (Psalm 42:10). The psalmist has already been mocked and heard words that feel like swords. If Jacob's words are daggers, the pain will increase.

From his place at the temple, Jacob speaks a few short words of consolation directly to the Nephite women. Without discounting their concerns and pain, Jacob tells the Nephite women that God will

---

40. There are 2 uses of guilt in the Old Testament (Deut 19:13, 21:9) and none in the New Testament. D&C 134:4 and Moses 6:54 speak of guilt, and the word is used in twelve verses in the Book of Mormon. But only Jacob and Enos personalize guilt and own it as their own.

"console you in your afflictions" (Jacob 3:1), and he encourages them to "lift up [their] heads" and "feast upon" God's "love" (Jacob 3:2). Thirsting for comfort from a living God, the psalmist has wept "tears" night and day, calling them "meat" as if the tears were food (Psalm 42:3). Jacob's suggestion of feasting connotes abundance and fullness in the best of ways, which is doubtless comforting for the Nephite women, especially if they were aware of Psalm 42/43 and the psalmist who has been eating the meat of pain and tears.

Jacob's description of the pain of the women in Jerusalem and their cries to God is powerful. It is also a fitting definition of lament. He assures the Nephite women that "the sobbings of their hearts ascend up to God" (Jacob 2:35). Their tears and pain have been heard. Jacob's assurances to the Nephite women include his vivid awareness that women in the Old World suffered similarly. In his sermon, Jacob declares that God has "seen the sorrow and heard the mourning of the daughters of my people in the land of Jerusalem, yea, and in all the lands of my people, because of the wickedness and abominations of their husbands" (Jacob 2:31). Both the Nephite women and the women from Jerusalem have "mourned," possibly in the same manner as the psalmist, weeping and lamenting and crying out to God, "O deliver me from the deceitful and unjust man" (Psalm 43:1). Notably, the psalmist has moved from vague plural enemies to focus specifically on a singular "unjust man," a "distinct enemy."[41] The Nephite women likely resonate with this verse when they cry out to God against their husbands.

Jacob promises the Nephite women that God will "console you in your afflictions, and he will *plead your cause*, and send down justice upon those who seek your destruction" (Jacob 3:1, my emphasis). These words certainly comfort the Nephite women, but Jacob is speaking in the psalmist's words. It is the psalmist who prays, "Judge me, O God, and *plead my cause* against an ungodly nation: O deliver me from the deceitful and unjust man" (Psalm 43:1, my emphasis). Jacob is the only person outside of the Hebrew Bible who says that God will

---

41. Staffan Olofsson, *As a Deer Longs for Flowing Streams: A Study of the Septuagint Version of Psalm 42–43 in its relation to the Hebrew text.* Vol. 1. (Göttingen, Germany, Vandenhoeck & Ruprecht, 2011), 66.

"plead [pronoun] cause." (Jacob 3:1)[42] While Jacob could be echoing the phrasing of one of the other eleven people in the Old Testament who speak of pleading their own or someone else's cause, he is not. Jacob and the psalmist in Psalm 42/43 are the only two people in scripture who are counting on God to "plead" someone's "cause," and who follow that phrasing with a statement about justice: the psalmist begs God to "deliver me from the deceitful and *unjust* man." Jacob promises the Nephite women that God will send "justice down" upon the Nephite men (Jacob 3:1). The echoes of Psalm 42/43 and Jacob's temple sermon may be how and why Enos knows that his father, Jacob, "was a just man" (Enos 1:1).

The relative uniqueness of the phrasing about pleading someone's cause, and the utter uniqueness of that phrase being followed with a reference to God's justice connects Psalm 42/43 to Jacob's temple sermon and Jacob's concern for women and children. Multiple images and echoes connect Enos with the same Psalm, and even more words and phrases connect Enos with his father, Jacob. Even so, it is stunning that no one in the Book of Mormon except for Enos and Jacob refer to their God as "my Maker"—a title for God that connects father to son on the precise point of Jacob's shame and Enos's repentance. The father and son meet, possibly only through written word, at a temple. Their words overlap, centering on the only emotion/feeling that Enos seems filled with at the beginning: his own guilt. By owning his guilt, Enos allows both his father's and his Father's words to sink into his heart. The words change him into a whole person, someone who "began to feel a desire for the welfare" of others, and someone who "began" to have unshaken faith.

Psalm 42/43, Jacob's sermons, and Enos's story triangulate in content and context and form a nexus around unjust men in general and one particular unjust man, someone who had a just man for his father and a penchant for hearing words that changed him. In the past is where Jacob stands at the temple, speaking supportive words to Nephite women about the justice of God. Jacob's words echo in Psalm 42/43

---

42. In D&C 124:75, God commands Vinson Knight to "plead the cause of the poor and the needy," which seems close but is not precisely parallel.

and echo again in Enos's narrative. Shared words point readers to a deer with feminine actions, a psalmist who thirsts for God and cries night and day, and a lament about an unjust man who mocks the psalmist saying, "Where is thy God?" The echoes may resonate with a man who has said something similar and is full of guilt, who has alienated multiple people in his life, perhaps nearly everyone, and who feels relatively empty and alone. He goes hunting in the forest, and he finds the words of his father weigh on his mind. That place becomes a temple to him. He prays and weeps for long hours, crying out to a merciful God for forgiveness, as desperate for God as an animal whose very life depends upon finding clear, flowing water.

7. Conclusion

The name, Enos, simply means "man," or, more specifically, "man in his frailty."[43] In other words, *Enos* is the title of a category. Perhaps readers think they know Enos because they do. Enos is a title that names everyone in general and no one in particular. Each reader believes they know *the* Enos because each reader is *an* Enos. Each reader is an individualized, particularized manifestation of humanity. Indeed, not only can everyone be an Enos, everyone must be an Enos.

When Enos begins this story, he is already a fallen person in a fallen world. That is difficult to see, however, without comparing him to other manifestations of fallen people. To become whole involves recognizing and owning personal guilt. It means allowing the words that have often been spoken to actually be heard. Before the words, this Enos is just a sinful hunter who feels lonely and empty inside. All he has is his gnawing hunger and his guilt. Hunting beasts could satiate a raw need for food, but if his hunger is metaphorical at all, if it is mixed up with the guilt he acknowledges as his own, then hunting beasts will not fix either the guilt or his hunger. And oh, how he hungers—so much hunger, so encompassing that it is expressed without bounds or

---

43. Judson Cornwall, and Stelman Smith, "Enos," *The Exhaustive Dictionary of Bible Names*. (Newberry, Florida: Bridge-Logos, 998): 51.

conditions. Human hunger is often expressed in terms of want. This Enos *needs*.

The Enos in the Book of Mormon may not record the content of his prayer for his own soul because he cannot. Enos is only a title for all humanity, and while any particular manifestation of Enos can learn from a prayer narrative about whom to approach in mighty prayer, how words provoke action and real consequences, and how answers may come, the content of that prayer cannot be shared in a way that will change another person's life (See chart: "Process of Prayer"). Each individual Enos must offer his or her own mighty prayer. All are unjust in their own ways. All have in some way created the pain of Psalm 42/43 for another. The answer is to call upon God, praying to a personal Maker for relief from the hunger, begging the Maker to unmake the sins and misdeeds that have left a trail of disconnection and pain and guilt.

When God answers his prayer, this Enos speaks. His one line of quotable, direct speech is a completely unclear question. When he asks, "Lord, how is it done?" he may be asking how sins are forgiven, how guilt is swept away, how he knows that his father is a just man, or how God hears his prayers when he raises his voice on high. Readers do not know because the text never says. From Enos's incomplete first sentence, his narrative has been calling our attention to such gaps and silences and lost words. While that sounds like a metaphor, it is not. The words of Enos 1:3 were edited in 1837 by Joseph Smith to remove extra words that seemed repetitious and convoluted. And yet, fixed with a simple mark of punctuation, the original wording forms a complete sentence and conveys a powerful message in the context of this paper. Enos says,

> "Behold, I went to hunt beasts in the forest and the words which I had often heard my father speak concerning eternal life and the joy of the saints. And the words of my father sunk deep into my heart, and I hungered" (Wording of original Book of Mormon, my punctuation).

It is an odd thing to say, but no less odd that other phrases this Enos uses. It seems that when he went to the forest to hunt beasts, he found something else: *his father's words*. He knew then that he should have been hunting those words—not beasts—all along.

The missing words point readers to the most obvious difference between Psalm 42/43 and the Enos text: Enos may be nearly silent in one, but God is silent in the other. The Psalm is about a pray-er and about a prayer, not because it is the story of prayer but because it is the prayer. Despite the common assessment, Enos's story is not really about a pray-er, and it is even less about three prayers. Psalm 42/43 ends with a repetitious refrain promising to continue praying until God's face is found. Enos's story does not. Much is vague, questionable, debatable, or lost in silence in Enos's story. What is not vague, questionable, debatable, or lost in silence is this: God.

Enos's words are missing because each Enos has his or her own prayer to pray. God's words are not missing because no matter which Enos hungers, no matter which Enos prays all day or cries all night or raises a personal voice on high so that it reaches the heavens, the answer is the same: "Enos, thy sins are forgiven thee, and thou shalt be blessed."

"I will tell you of a wrestle I had before God," says Enos. He addresses you because you are him and so am I.

Enos is our name.

Table 1: Typical structural breakdown for Enos 1:1–18.[44]

Section		Reference
1	Prayer for self	Enos 1:1–8
2	Prayer for own people (Nephites)	Enos 1:9–11
3	Prayer for his brethren (Lamanites)	Enos 1:12–18

---

44. See, for example, "Book of Enos," Guide to the Scriptures, https://www.churchofjesuschrist.org/study/scriptures/gs/enos-son-of-jacob.

Table 2: Process of prayer

	Prayer 1 for "mine own soul"	Prayer 2 for "the welfare of my brethren, the Nephites"	Prayer 3 for "the welfare of my brethren, the Lamanites"
Transition into prayer	¹ Behold, it came to pass . . .	⁹ Now, it came to pass . . .	¹² And it came to pass that after . . .
Words that provoke action	³ Behold, . . . the words which I had often heard my father speak concerning eternal life, and the joy of the saints, sunk deep into my heart.	(9 cont.) . . . when I had heard these words . . .	¹¹ And after I, Enos, had heard these words, . . .
Action/ reaction to words	⁴ And my soul hungered; and I kneeled down before my Maker, and I cried unto him in mighty prayer and supplication . . .	(9 cont.) . . . I began to feel a desire for the welfare of my brethren, the Nephites; . . .	(11 cont.) . . . my faith began to be unshaken in the Lord; . . .
Prayer	(4 cont.) . . . I cried unto him in might prayer and supplication for mine own soul; and all the day long did I cry unto him; yea, and when the night came I did still raise my voice high that it reached the heavens.	(9 cont.) . . . wherefore, I did pour out my whole soul unto God for them.	(11 cont.) . . . I prayed unto him with many long strugglings for my brethren, the Lamanites. (12 cont.) . . . after I had prayed and labored with all diligence, the Lord said unto me: . . .
Description of Answer	⁵ And there came a voice unto me, saying: . . .	¹⁰ And while I was thus struggling in the spirit, . . .	(12 cont.) . . . the Lord said unto me: . . .

	Prayer 1 for "mine own soul"	Prayer 2 for "the welfare of my brethren, the Nephites"	Prayer 3 for "the welfare of my brethren, the Lamanites"
Answer	**(5 cont.)** . . . Enos, thy sins are forgiven thee, and thou shalt be blessed.	**(10 cont.)** . . . behold, the voice of the Lord came into my mind again, saying: I will visit thy brethren according to their diligence in keeping my commandments. I have given unto them this land, and it is a holy land; and I curse it not save it be for the cause of iniquity; wherefore, I will visit thy brethren according as I have said; and their transgressions will I bring down with sorrow upon their own heads.	**(12 cont.)** . . . the Lord said unto me: I will grant unto thee according to thy desires, because of thy faith.
Aftermath/ continue conversation/ etc.	**6** And I, Enos, knew that God could not lie; wherefore, my guilt was swept away. **7** And I said: Lord, how is it done? **8** And he said unto me: Because of thy faith in Christ, whom thou hast never before heard nor seen. And many years pass away before he shall manifest himself in the flesh; wherefore, go to, thy faith hath made thee whole.		

Prayer 3: Prayer for Future (Lamanites & Records)

Far past			**15** Wherefore, I knowing that the Lord God was able to preserve our records, I cried unto him continually, **for he had said unto me: Whatsoever thing ye shall ask in faith, believing that ye shall receive in the name of Christ, ye shall receive it.**
			Sometime in the past, God has said this to Enos.
Past	**11** And after I, Enos, had heard these words, my faith began to be unshaken in the Lord; and I prayed unto him with many long strugglings for my brethren, the Lamanites.	**13** And now behold, this was the desire which I desired of him—that if it should so be, that my people, the Nephites, should fall into transgression, and by any means be destroyed, and the Lamanites should not be destroyed, that the Lord God would preserve a record of my people, the Nephites; even if it so be by the power of his holy arm, that it might be brought forth at some future day unto the Lamanites, that, perhaps, they might be brought unto salvation—	**15 Wherefore, I knowing that the Lord God was able to preserve our records, I cried unto him continually,** for he had said unto me: Whatsoever thing ye shall ask in faith, believing that ye shall receive in the name of Christ, ye shall receive it.
	After Nephite prayer, Enos prayed for Lamanites.	This is what Enos's desire was that God answered with a "yes" in verse 12. This is the "Lamanite" prayer.	Because of what God said in the past, Enos cries continually (ie, with many long strugglings)

	Present		
Present	12 And it came to pass that after I had prayed and labored with all diligence, the Lord said unto me: I will grant unto thee according to thy desires, because of thy faith.	14 For at the present our strugglings were vain in restoring them to the true faith. And they swore in their wrath that, if it were possible, they would destroy our records and us, and also all the traditions of our fathers.	16 And I had faith, and I did cry unto God that he would preserve the records; and he covenanted with me that he would bring them forth unto the Lamanites in his own due time.
	Answer to Lamanite prayer is: I will grant unto thee according to thy desires, because of thy faith	Present time: Lamanites won't listen at all to gospel. They want to destroy Nephites and their records.	Answer to Lamanite prayer is that yes, God will preserve records. He covenants to bring them forth to latter day Lamanites.
Covenant			17 And I, Enos, knew it would be according to the covenant which he had made; wherefore my soul did rest. 18 And the Lord said unto me: Thy fathers have also required of me this thing; and it shall be done unto them according to their faith; for their faith was like unto thine.

Enos 1:1–18: A Critical Text

1 Behold,[1] it came to pass[2] that I, Enos,[3] knowing[4] my father,[5] that he

---

1. Enos uses the word "behold" three further times in his writings—in verse 3, in verse 10, and in verse 13. It is never again used with "it came to pass."

2. Enos uses "it came to pass" less frequently than most Nephite authors, only six times in this narrative-heavy chapter. It appears here, and then in verses 9, 12, 19, 21, and 25. It is to be noted that it appears just three times within the narrative of Enos's wrestle.

3. Enos uses this first-person "I, Enos" formula five times: in the present verse, and then in verses 6, 11, 17, and 19. The only time it appears along with an "it came to pass" formula again is verse 19, which marks a strong transition from the story of the wrestle to the remainder of the chapter—effectively dividing the Book of Enos in two. It might be noted that the name "Enos" is first biblical, the name of Adam's grandson through Seth (see Genesis 4:26; 5:6–11; 1 Chronicles 1:1; Luke 3:38 (see also D&C 107:44, 53; Moses 6:3–18). The Nephite Enos is mentioned outside of his own book only in Jacob 7:27 and Jarom 1:1. In the Bible, the name "Enos" means "mortal."

4. Enos will again use the gerundive "knowing" in verse 15, in a rather similar fashion.

5. Enos never uses his father's name, but he does refer to him again as "my father" in verse 4. He refers also to "the traditions of our fathers" in verse 14, and God speaks to Enos of his "fathers" in verse 18. In verse 25, he refers to "our father Lehi," and in verse 27 he quotes the Redeemer as speaking of his own father.

was a just man[6] (for he taught me in his language,[7] and also in the nurture and admonition[8] of the Lord[9]—and blessed[10] be the name[11] of my

6. The phrase "was a just man" appears only once in the Old Testament, in the famous description of Noah, who "was a just man and perfect in his generations" (Genesis 6:9). All other references to "a just man" or to "just men" in the Old Testament appear in Proverbs and Ecclesiastes (some six times). The phrase "was a just man" appears twice in the New Testament, in a description of Joseph, the father of Jesus— "Joseph her husband, being a just man" (Matthew 1:19)—and in a clearly relevant passage about Herod: "Herod feared John, knowing that he was a just man" (Mark 6:20). Elsewhere in the New Testament, Pilate's wife calls Jesus "that just man" (Matthew 27:19), and Cornelius is described as "a just man" (Acts 10:22); and there are two references to "just men" (Luke 20:20; Hebrews 12:23). In the Book of Mormon, the phrase "just man" or "just men" seems focused principally on leaders, both governmental and ecclesiastical. Amaleki describes himself as "knowing King Benjamin to be a just man" in a clearly relevant passage (Omni 1:25), and Mormon himself describes Benjamin as "a just man" in Mosiah 2:4 (referring in the same verse also to the "just men" Benjamin appointed as teachers). Limhi too is "a just man" in Mosiah 19:17. Alma claims that only "just men" could make good kings (Mosiah 23:8)—a point directly echoed by Mosiah (Mosiah 29:13)—and then consecrates only "just men" as priests (Mosiah 23:17). Lamoni calls the Nephite missionaries "just men" as he defends them to his father (Alma 20:15). Shiblon is called "a just man" in Alma 63:2 when he takes office in the church, and Lachoneus, a later governor, is also "a just man" (3 Nephi 3:12), just as is Nephi as a keeper of the record (see 3 Nephi 8:1).

7. It is a Book of Mormon idea that one is taught in another's language (see Omni 1:18; Mosiah 1:2, 4; 9:1). It seems likely, in addition to passages that use this same formula, that there is a deliberate echo here of 1 Nephi 1:1: "I was taught somewhat in all the learning of my father."

8. This phrase contains a clear allusion to Ephesians 6:4, which contains an injunction to "fathers" to "bring [their children] up in the nurture and admonition of the Lord." Only these two passages in all of scripture use the word "nurture," and the word "admonition" is strikingly rare—appearing in the Bible only in two other passages (see 1 Corinthians 10:11; Titus 3:10) and in the Book of Mormon only in one other passage (see 2 Nephi 4:13).

9. The first title Enos uses for God is, here, "the Lord," albeit in a formulaic phrase apparently tied to Ephesians 6:4 (see the note on "nurture and admonition" in this same verse). He will, though, use the title "Lord" again in verses 7, 10, 11, 12, 18, 23. By the end of the present verse, however, he will speak instead of "God." The latter title appears several times in Enos's text, in verses 1, 2, 6, 9, 16, 20, 23, and 26. A combination of these two titles, "the Lord God," appears in verses 13 and 15. Three times Enos will refer to "Christ" (in verses 8, 15, and 26), once to the "Redeemer" (in verse 27), and once to God as "Father" (also in verse 27). In verse 4, Enos refers to God as his "Maker."

10. Enos will twice more refer to blessedness—in verse 5, where God pronounces Enos himself "blessed," and in verse 27, when the Redeemer calls Enos "blessed" in inviting him into eternal bliss.

11. The only other "name" to which Enos refers is "the name of Christ" in verse 15.

God[12] for it!), **2** and I will tell you[13] of the wrestle[14] which I had before God[15] before that[16] I received[17] a remission of my sins.[18] //

---

12. Blessing God's name is a traditional gesture. It appears ten times in the Old Testament, primarily in the poetic books (see Nehemiah 9:5; Job 1:21; Psalms 72:19; 96:2; 100:4; 103:1; 113:2; 145:1, 21; Daniel 2:20), but never in the New Testament. The gesture appears another eight times in the Book of Mormon (see Alma 7:4; 19:12; 26:8, 36 [twice]; 57:35; 3 Nephi 4:32; 11:17). Only once in the Bible is the gesture used with the word "God" (rather than "the Lord" or the simple possessive pronoun "his"), in Daniel 2:20. In the Book of Mormon, however, it is usually *God's* name, rather than the Lord's name, that is blessed (the only exceptions being the two instances in Third Nephi, one blessing the name "of the Lord God Almighty, the Most High God," the other the name "of the Most High God"). Most of the Book of Mormon instances of the gesture use the imperative mood, as does Enos ("blessed *be*," rather than "blessed *is*"), with the exceptions being Alma 26:36 and Alma 57:35. Only a few of the other Book of Mormon instances of the gesture use the first-person possessive pronoun ("my" or "our God"), as Enos does—Alma 26:36 (twice) using "my God" and Alma 26:8 and Alma 57:35 using "our God." As for the title "God" itself, see the note on "Lord" earlier in this same verse.

13. Although the phrase "I will tell you" appears elsewhere in scripture, it never introduces a story. This is a use of the phrase unique to Enos.

14. Wrestling is surprisingly uncommon in scripture. It appears in the story of Naphtali's birth in Genesis 30:8 ("And Rachel said, With great wrestlings have I wrestled with my sister, and I have prevailed: and she called his name Naphtali"). It appears of course in the story of Jacob's wrestle in Genesis 32:24–25 ("And Jacob was left alone; and there wrestled a man with him until the breaking of the day"). It appears once in the New Testament: "For we wrestle not against flesh and blood, but against principalities, against powers," etc. (Ephesians 6:12). And then, in addition to the present verse, it appears only once elsewhere in the Book of Mormon, in Alma 8:10: "Nevertheless Alma labored much in the spirit, wrestling with God in mighty prayer."

15. In the Book of Mormon, when an action is done (rather than just an attitude assumed) "before God," it is usually either standing or walking (as in "standing uprightly"). Enos's wrestle before God is, of course, entirely unique. On the title "God," see the note on "Lord" in verse 1.

16. The phrase "before that" was changed to simply "before" for the 1837 edition, and it has read that way in all subsequent printed editions.

17. Only once in the Bible does one "receive" a "remission" of sins—in Acts 10:43. This formula, though, appears some times in the Book of Mormon, in addition to the present verse (see Mosiah 3:13; 4:3, 11; 38:8; 3 Nephi 7:25; 12:2; 30:2).

18. The phrase "remission of [one's] sins," with a possessive pronoun, shows up with some frequency in scripture, but so does the phrase "remission of sins," without a possessive pronoun. The two variations show up in the New Testament some eight times (neither shows up in the Old Testament). The formula with the possessive pronoun is predominant and appears in Matthew 26:28; Mark 1:4; Luke 3:3; 24:47; Acts 2:38; 10:43; and Romans 3:25. The formula with the possessive pronoun shows up only in Luke 1:77, which speaks of giving "knowledge of salvation unto [the Lord's] people by the remission of their sins." Both variations appear in the Book of Mormon as well, though the formula without the possessive pronoun does not appear before Third Nephi. It shows up in 3 Nephi 1:23; 7:16, 23; Moroni 3:3; 8:11, 25, 26—generally in contexts where the remission of sins simply is not tied to a particular person. The formula with the possessive pronoun here dominates, however, showing up twenty times. It appears twice before Enos, in 2 Nephi 25:26; 31:17; and then it appears seventeen times afterward: Mosiah 3:13; 4:3, 11, 12, 20, 26; 15:11; Alma

3 Behold,[19] I went to hunt[20] beasts in the forest,[21] and[22] the words[23] which

---

4:14; 7:6; 12:34; 13:16; 30:16; 38:8; 3 Nephi 7:25; 12:2; 30:2; Moroni 10:33. It is of interest that only one of these passages uses the first-person singular possessive pronoun, "my"—Alma 38:8—where it also appears in a kind of conversion narrative. Note also that Enos will refer again to "sins" only in verse 5, where they are "forgiven."

19. See the note on "behold" in verse 1.

20. Hunting is not much mentioned in scripture. The verb "to hunt" appears eighteen times and the noun "hunter" five times in the Old Testament, neither of these in the New Testament at all, and the verb twelve times and the noun twice in the Book of Mormon—and nowhere else in Restoration scripture. Nimrod is "a mighty hunter before the Lord" (Genesis 10:9), and Esau hunts (see Genesis 27:5, 27, 30). Leviticus 17:13 records one law about hunting (and is the only passage outside of Enos that specifically mentions hunting beasts). David describes Saul as hunting him, twice (see 1 Samuel 24:11; 26:20). Job accuses God of hunting him (see Job 10:16), and God eventually responds by asking Job whether he can "hunt the prey for the lion" (Job 38:39). Hunting is used as imagery in a psalm (see Psalms 140:11) and in two proverbs (see Proverbs 6:5, 26), but one proverb also refers to actual hunting (see Proverbs 12:27). It's an image in several prophetic books (see Jeremiah 16:16; Lamentations 4:18; Ezekiel 13:18, 20, 21; Micah 7:2). Ten of the Book of Mormon's twelve uses of the verb refer to armies hunting out their enemies: Mosiah 17:18; Alma 25:8, 9, 12; Helaman 3:16; 6:37; 15:12; Mormon 2:20; 8:2, 7. Only in Ether 10:19 is there another reference to hunting proper (though the phrase there is "to hunt food" rather than "to hunt beasts"), where "Lib also himself became a great hunter." Ether 2:1 before that point refers to a valley named after Nimrod, "being called after the mighty hunter." Nephi of course does a good deal of hunting with his brothers in First Nephi, but the verb "to hunt" is never used—instead "to slay wild beasts."

21. The word "forest" is in the singular in the printer's manuscript (the original manuscript is not extant for this verse), and it appeared in the singular in printed editions until 1905, when a typesetter replaced the word with the plural "forests." It has been printed in the plural in Latter-day Saint editions since. Forests are not often mentioned in the Book of Mormon. Nephi does say that he found "beasts in the forest of every kind" upon arrival in the New World (1 Nephi 18:25), but the remainder of his several references to forests come in quotations of Isaiah (see 2 Nephi 19:18; 20:18, 19, 34; 27:28). Limhi speaks of "the beasts of the forest" in one passage, poetically (Mosiah 8:21), and this may be connected to the fact that his land was bordered by "the forest that was near the waters of Mormon," referred to in Mosiah 18:30, or to the fact that there were "forests" for his people to hide in as they waited for their enemies (Mosiah 20:8). No other forests are mentioned until Jesus Christ quotes a passage from Micah that refers to forests (see 3 Nephi 20:16; 21:12). And then the last reference to a forest is in Ether 10:19, where "the land southward . . . was covered with animals of the forest." In all this, it seems significant that the only forests mentioned are in the land of Nephi, where Enos dwells.

22. Because of the difficulty of the earliest extant reading of this verse (in the printer's manuscript—the original manuscript is not extant for this verse), Royal Skousen suggests emending the text by adding "I remembered" after "and" here. See Skousen, *Analysis*, 1073–75.

23. Enos will refer to "words" in the plural three more times, always with reference to words that he "heard" (once later in this same verse, and then in verses 9 and 11). In verse 26, he refers to "the word" that he must "declare."

I had often²⁴ heard my father²⁵ speak²⁶ concerning eternal life²⁷ and the joy of the saints²⁸—and the words²⁹ of my father³⁰ sunk deep into my heart,³¹

---

24. This passage is the only one in scripture in which something is "often heard." Malachi 3:16 (quoted in 3 Nephi 24:16) is the only other passage where "often" is connected to the verb "to speak." No other passage in scripture connects "often" to "words." Enos's formula here, at least in light of the word "often," is strikingly unique.

25. See the note on "father" in verse 1.

26. There is no direct echo of Enos's phrasing here ("the words which I had often heard my father speak") elsewhere in scripture, but there is some general similarity with Nephi's reflection on his own father's words in 1 Nephi 10:16.

27. It is possible to hear an echo of John 6:68, "thou hast the words of eternal life," here, though the echo is distant. The phrase "concerning eternal life" is wholly unique to this passage. Although it seems unlikely that Enos means to refer to a specific passage from his father's writings, it is worth noting that Jacob twice refers to "eternal life" in his contributions to the small plates; see 2 Nephi 10:23; Jacob 6:11. It is worth noting that Enos refers to "eternity" in verse 23.

28. The phrase "the joy of the saints" is unique to this passage, but Psalm 132 twice speaks of "saints" who "shout" or "shout aloud for joy" (Psalms 132:9, 16). Jacob, in his small-plates contributions, directly connects "joy" to "saints." In 2 Nephi 9:18, he says of "the righteous, the saints of the Holy One of Israel," that they "shall inherit the kingdom of God, which was prepared for them from the foundation of the world, and their joy shall be full forever." In the next verse, he goes on to explain further that "God, the Holy One of Israel . . . delivereth his saints from that awful monster the devil, and death and hell, and that lake of fire and brimstone, which is endless torment." Jacob refers in a few other passages either to joy or to saints, without connected them. A few references to joy appear in his quotation of Isaiah 51, for instance (see 2 Nephi 8:3, 11). He refers to joy also in Jacob 4:3, and the word "joy" shows up in Zenos's allegory of the olive tree, which he quotes, in Jacob 5:60. He refers just one other time to "saints," in 2 Nephi 9:43.

29. See the note on "words" earlier in this same verse.

30. The phrase "and the words of my father" here appear in the printer's manuscript and in the 1830 edition of the Book of Mormon. (The original manuscript is not extant for this verse.) Joseph Smith crossed out the phrase in the printer's manuscript in preparation for the 1837 edition (neglecting, actually, to cross out "and," although his intention was understood by the printer). The phrase has since failed to appear in printed editions of the Book of Mormon. The phrase "the words of my father" is unique to the Book of Mormon, and there is almost exclusively used by Nephi to refer to Lehi's words (as in 1 Nephi 8:29, 34; 10:17; 11:5) or by Jacob to refer to the same (as in 2 Nephi 6:3). The one exception is in Moroni 7:1, where Moroni writes "a few of the words of my father."

31. The use of "to sink" with "deep" is unique to this passage, as is the image of sinking "into one's heart." The only somewhat similar phrasing in scripture comes from Luke 9:44, where Jesus says this to his disciples: "Let these sayings sink down into your ears." This phrase marks the only time Enos uses the word "heart."

4 and my soul[32] hungered.[33] And I kneeled down before[34] my Maker,[35] and I cried[36] unto him in mighty prayer[37] and supplication[38] for mine own soul.[39] And all the day long[40]

---

32. Enos uses the word "soul" just four times—in the present verse twice, in verse 9, and finally in verse 17. The several instances of the word seem to be linked.

33. The Psalms and the Proverbs refer to "the hungry soul" (Psalms 107:9; Proverbs 27:7), but these seem to refer to the literal hunger of the body. In 3 Nephi 20:8, though, Christ promises to the one who eat and drink of the sacramental emblems that "his soul shall never hunger."

34. Only one other passage in scripture has someone "kneeling down . . . before" someone, and it is before "all the congregation of Israel" (in 2 Chronicles 6:13). The verb "to kneel" without "down" appears with "before" in Psalms 95:6, where there also appears "the Lord our maker." The coupling of "to kneel" with "down" appears, though, only seven times in the Book of Mormon. This is the first, and the next appears only in Third Nephi. Enos is relatively unique. (For other Book of Mormon uses of the phrase, see 3 Nephi 17:13; 19:6, 16, 17; Moroni 4:2.)

35. God is referred to as a "maker" some sixteen times in the Old Testament (in a particularly relevant text in Psalms 95:6) and just once in the New Testament. The term is used in the Book of Mormon a few times—once in a quotation of Isaiah by Jacob (see 2 Nehi 8:13), and then a couple of other times by Jacob (see 2 Nephi 9:40; Jacob 2:6). It does not appear again until Helaman 1:11, where it is the figure by whom the Gadianton robbers swear. It appears once more in Third Nephi, in another quotation of Isaiah (see 3 Nephi 22:5). On titles for God in Enos, see the note on "Lord" in verse 1.

36. "To cry" is the verb Enos uses most consistently for prayer in his story. He uses it again in this same verse, and then again in verses 15 and 16.

37. The phrase "mighty prayer" never occurs in the Bible. It appears before this point in the Book of Mormon only in 2 Nephi 4:24, but it appears afterward in a few passages: Alma 6:6; 8:10 (where it is coupled with "wrestling"); 3 Nephi 27:1; Moroni 2:2. Enos will use the verb "to pray" in verses 11 and 12. In both cases, the verb is accompanied by some indication of a wrestle—with "many long strugglings" in verse 11, and with "labored with all diligence" in verse 12.

38. The word "supplication" occurs sixty times in the Bible, fifty-three of them in the Old Testament (most frequently in 1 Kings—in the dedication of the temple—and in Psalms). The word is far less frequent in the Book of Mormon, appearing just five times. Enos's use marks the first instance, and then it appears in Alma 7:3; 31:10; 3 Nephi 4:10; Moroni 6:9.

39. The phrase "mine own soul" is unique to this passage, although "his own soul" or "their own souls" appears more than twenty times in scripture (twenty times in the Bible, and some three times in the Book of Mormon). See also the note on "soul" earlier in this same verse.

40. The phrase "all the day long" appears twelve times in the Old Testament, once in the New Testament (explicitly quoting the Old Testament), and then twelve times in the Book of Mormon. Nephi uses it to describe his praise of God during suffering in a passage parallel to a story of the brother of Jared (see 1 Nephi 18:16; Ether 6:9), and he uses it to describe God's patiently reaching out for his people (see 2 Nephi 28:32). Jacob uses it in Zenos's allegory of the olive tree (see Jacob 5:47) and harks back to it twice in his subsequent comments (see Jacob 6:4, 7). Abinadi later uses it to predict the howling of the wicked (see Mosiah 12:4), and Mormon says of the people of Limhi that they cried "all the day long" to God for deliverance (Mosiah 21:14). Ammon tells his companions that they labored "all the day long" (Alma 26:5), but Alma worries about the wicked who desire evil "all the day long" (Alma 41:5). Most relevant of all, perhaps, is that Mormon speaks

did I cry[41] unto him—yea,[42] and when the night came,[43] I did still raise my voice[44] high[45] that it reached the heavens.[46] **5** And there came a voice[47] unto me, saying, "Enos,[48] thy sins[49] are forgiven thee,[50]

---

of his love for his people in prayer: "my soul has been poured out in prayer unto my God all the day long for them" (Mormon 3:12).

41. See the note on "cried" earlier in this same verse.

42. This is the only time Enos uses the emphatic "yea."

43. There are echoes of this phrase later in the Book of Mormon. Ether 6:9 says of the Jaredites in the barges that "when the night came, they did not cease to praise the Lord"—this right after a use of the phrase "all the day long." Also, relevant and by way of direct contrast, the Jaredites at the end of their destruction, are described in this way: "and when the night came again they did rend the air with their cries, and their howlings, and their mournings" (Ether 15:17). The phrase "when the night came" is used another seven times in the Book of Mormon, without obvious relevance.

44. The phrase "to raise one's voice" is strikingly infrequent in scripture. It never appears in the Bible, and it appears in the Book of Mormon just three times. Apart from the present verse, it appears in Mosiah 24:12; 25:10—and in both other instances, it is also in reference to praising God. It might be noted that Enos's voice in this verse will be answered with "a voice" in the next verse. The only other mention of "voice" in Enos is in verse 10.

45. The idea of a voice being "high" appears in the Old Testament in just two passages—in 2 Chronicles 20:19 and Isaiah 58:4—and just in one other passage in the Book of Mormon, from Nephi's psalm: 2 Nephi 4:24.

46. The phrase "reached the heavens" echoes Old Testament passages—the top of the tower of Babel (see Genesis 11:4), Jacob's ladder (see Genesis 28:12), the rage of Israel described by Oded (see 2 Chronicles 28:9), the Lord's judgment according to Jeremiah (see Jeremiah 51:9), the tree of Daniel's vision (see Daniel 4:11, 20, 22), and the sins of Babylon in John's vision (see Revelation 18:5). This passage in Enoch marks the only instance of the formula in the Book of Mormon.

47. The phrase "there came a voice" is biblical. It appears once in the Old Testament, in the story of Elijah's peculiar visit to Sinai (see 1 Kings 19:13). It then appears five times in the New Testament, in Mark 1:11 (the annunciation at Jesus's baptism), Luke 9:35 (the annunciation on the Mount of Transfiguration), Acts 10:13 (during Peter's vision about extending the gospel to gentiles), 2 Peter 1:17 (in a reference back to the Mount of Transfiguration), and Revelation 16:17 (at the moment that apocalyptic terror reaches its climax). It appears in the Book of Mormon just three times outside of Enos: twice in the story of the Lamanite conversion in Helaman, once in a threat and once in a word of comfort (see Helaman 5:29, 46), and then once in 3 Nephi 10:3, when the voice of Christ speaks from the darkness to the fallen children of Lehi. See also the note on "voice" in verse 4.

48. This is the only time Enos's name appears in the Book of Enos outside of an "I, Enos" formula. See the note on "I, Enos" in verse 1.

49. See the note on "remission of my sins" in verse 2.

50. The phrase "thy sins are forgiven thee" directly echoes the story of the palsied man's healing (and the subsequent controversy over Jesus's ability to heal him). See Matthew 9:2, 5; Mark 2:5, 9; Luke 5:20, 23. It does not show up in the Bible apart from that thrice-repeated story, and this is its only occurrence in the Book of Mormon.

and thou shalt be blessed."[51] **6** And I, Enos,[52] knew[53] that God[54] could not lie[55]; wherefore,[56] my guilt[57] was swept away.[58] **7** And I saith,[59] "Lord,[60]

---

51. The future prediction of "thou shalt be blessed" is somewhat unexpected. As other instances of the phrase make clear (see 2 Nephi 1:9; 4:11; Alma 50:20), this has a strong bearing on the future. What appears more or less universally by way of blessing in such direct experiences with the voice of the Lord in the Book of Mormon is "blessed art thou," instead. See, for example, 1 Nephi 2:1, 19; 11:6; Mosiah 26:15, 17; Alma 8:15; 50:20; Helaman 10:4. See also the note on "blessed" in verse 1.

52. See the note on "I, Enos," in verse 1.

53. The phrase "and I, Enos, knew" reappears in verse 17.

54. See the note on "Lord" in verse 1.

55. The question of whether God can lie is raised a few times in the Book of Mormon. This is a central idea in the parallel discourses of Alma to the people to Ammonihah and to his son Corianton; see Alma 12:23; 42:5. It is also addressed in Ether 3:12 by the brother of Jared. All of these texts seem in a particularly important way to rely on Genesis 3:4–5.

56. This is Enos's first use of "wherefore." He uses it another five times: in verses 8, 9, 10, 15, and 17.

57. This is Enos's only reference to "guilt," but it is perhaps worth noting that Enos's father Jacob refers with some frequency to guilt. He mentions it in 2 Nephi 9:14, 46 (twice); and Jacob 6:9. A full seventh of the Book of Mormon's references to guilt thus appear in the writings or teachings of Jacob.

58. There are eight references to sweeping in the Bible—to rivers sweeping people away (see Judges 5:21), to "a sweeping rain which leaveth no food" (Proverbs 28:3), to destruction being an act of sweeping "with the besom of destruction" (Isaiah 14:23), to hail sweeping away "the refuge of lies" (Isaiah 28:17), to "valiant men swept away" (Jeremiah 46:15), to the swept house into which demons go for residence (see Matthew 12:44; Luke 11:25), and to the sweeping of the woman who lost a piece of silver (see Luke 15:8). The image is much more frequent in the Book of Mormon. It appears before Enos in only two passages—in a quotation of Isaiah's passage about "the besom of destruction" (2 Nephi 24:23), and in Zenos's allegory of the olive tree, where the lord of the vineyard announces that he will "sweep away the bad" from the vineyard (Jacob 5:66). It appears after Enos's use, however, some thirteen times, every one of them in a context of war or destruction: Jarom 1:3, 7; Alma 44:18; 49:22; Helaman 11:10; Mormon 4:18; 5:7; Ether 2:8, 9, 10 (twice); 14:18, 27. Nowhere else is *guilt* swept away.

59. The present-tense "saith" was replaced with the past-tense "said" in the 1837 edition, and it has appeared as "said" in all subsequent editions. The simple phrase "and I said" (to which "and I saith" was edited), without a prepositional phrase (like "unto him") following, appears fewer than thirty times in scripture. It appears a few times in the historical and poetic books of the Old Testament, but it primarily appears in that volume in the prophets, in visionary experiences with God or some divine intermediary (see Jeremiah 1:11, 13; 3:7, 19; 24:3; Amos 7:8; 8:2; Micah 3:1; Zechariah 3:5; 4:2, 5, 13; 5:6). It appears just three times in the New Testament, always in the Book of Acts when Paul is describing his encounter with the risen Christ (see Acts 22:10, 19; 26:15). In the Book of Mormon, it appears elsewhere only in Nephi's visionary experiences—see 1 Nephi 11:3, 5; 13:2; 17:9.

60. See the note on "Lord" in verse 1.

how is it done?"[61] **8** And he saith[62] unto me,[63] "Because of thy faith[64] in Christ,[65] whom thou hast not[66] heard nor seen.[67] And many years passeth[68] away[69] before that[70] he shall manifest himself in the[71] flesh.[72]

---

61. This question, "how is it done?" is entirely unique to this passage in scripture.

62. Here again, the present-tense "saith" was replaced with the past-tense "said" in the 1837 edition, and it has appeared as "said" in all subsequent editions.

63. This exact phrasing, "and he saith unto me," appears elsewhere only in the Book of Revelation (see Revelation 17:15; 19:9; 22:10). The altered text, "and he said unto me," appears much more frequently in scripture, although it should be noted that it appears in the New Testament also only in the Book of Revelation (see Revelation 10:9, 11; 19:10; 21:5, 6; 22:6) and in passages where Paul describes his visionary encounters with God (see Acts 22:8, 21; 2 Corinthians 12:9). The adjusted phrase appears some fourteen other times in the Book of Mormon and, without exception, it is used to report on some kind of divine (or supposedly divine) communication. See 1 Nephi 11:10, 14, 16, 18; 12:9; 13:3, 23; 14:10; Mosiah 3:2, 3; Alma 20:5; 30:53; 36:9; Helaman 14:27.

64. The phrase "because of thy faith" is unique to the Book of Mormon. It appears, of course, just a few verses later, in verse 12. It also appears in 1 Nephi 2:19 and Ether 3:9. The similar "because of your faith" is also unique to the Book of Mormon, where it appears just in Helaman 5:47; 3 Nephi 17:20; Moroni 7:41. This verse marks the first time Enos uses the word "faith," but he goes on to use it another nine times—once more in the present verse, and then in verses 11, 12, 14, 15, 16, 18 (twice), and 20.

65. The phrase "faith in Christ" appears in the New Testament four times, in Acts 24:24; Galatians 3:26; Colossians 1:4; 2:5. It then appears eleven times in the Book of Mormon—first in 2 Nephi 33:7 and Jacob 7:3 before it appears here, and then in Alma 25:16; 44:3; Helaman 5:41; 15:9; Moroni 7:25, 32, 39; 10:4. This verse marks the first use of "Christ" in Enos, but it is used again in verses 15 and 26. See also the note on "Lord" in verse 1.

66. Joseph Smith replaced "not" with "never before" in the printer's manuscript in preparation for the 1837 edition. The text reads "not" in the 1830 edition. It has appeared, however, with "never before" in every edition since 1837.

67. The closest thing to an echo in this phrasing is a possible relationship with John 5:37: "Ye have neither heard his voice at any time, nor seen his shape."

68. The conjugation of "to pass" for a singular subject ("passeth") was replaced with a conjugation for a plural subject ("pass") in the 1837 edition. It has appeared in the latter form in every subsequent printed edition.

69. The phrase "many years passeth away" is unique to this passage, with nothing akin to it appearing elsewhere. The phrase "many years" of course appears many times, especially prominent in the Book of Mormon (where the most frequent formula is "the space of many years").

70. The phrase "before that" was changed to simply "before" for the 1837 edition, and it has read that way in all subsequent printed editions.

71. The word "the" appears in the printer's manuscript only superlinearly, addedly belatedly (although how belatedly isn't clear) by Oliver Cowdery. It has appeared in every printed edition. Royal Skousen conjectures that it was present in the original manuscript (which is not extant for this verse) and that Oliver Cowdery corrected a mistaken omission when he added "the" superlinearly.

72. This formula, "manifest himself in the flesh," seems to derive from the New Testament, where it (or something like it) appears just twice. 2 Corinthians 4:11 speaks of the idea "that the life also of Jesus might be made manifest in our mortal flesh." 1 Timothy 3:16, somewhat less

Wherefore,[73] go to it.[74] Thy faith[75] hath made thee whole."[76] // **9** Now, it came to pass[77] that when I had heard these words,[78] I began[79] to feel a desire[80] for the welfare[81] of my brethren,[82]

---

complexly, says that "God was manifest in the flesh." In the Book of Mormon, the formula appears five times outside of Enos. Jacob says in 2 Nephi 6:9 that "the Lord God, the Holy One of Israel, should manifest himself unto them [Jews] in the flesh." Nephi later, in 2 Nephi 25:12, says that "the Only Begotten of the Father . . . shall manifest himself unto them [the Jews] in the flesh." Nephi uses the formula twice while addressing his own descendants: "there will be no more doctrine given until after he shall manifest himself unto you in the flesh, and when he shall manifest himself unto you in the flesh, the things which he shall say unto you shall ye observe to do" (2 Nephi 32:6). Finally, Jacob uses the formula again in Jacob 4:11, referring to the possibility of gaining "hope of glory in [Christ] before he manifesteth himself in the flesh." It is worth underscoring that all these instances of the formula appear in Nephi and Jacob before Enos. Enos provides the last use of it.

73. See the note on "wherefore" in verse 6.

74. The word "it" appears in the printer's manuscript (the original manuscript is not extant for this verse) and in the 1830 edition. Joseph Smith removed the word in preparation for the 1837 edition, and it has never appeared in print editions since that time. The phrase "go to it" is entirely unique to this passage. The simpler command, "Go to," appears some eight times in the Old Testament (see Genesis 11:3, 4, 7; 38:16; 2 Kings 5:5; Ecclesiastes 2:1; Isaiah 5:5; Jeremiah 18:11) and just twice in the New Testament (see James 4:13; 5:1). Outside of Enos (and 2 Nephi 15:5's quotation of Isaiah), it appears just in the allegory of the olive tree (twice; see Jacob 5:61, 71) and one passage in Ether (see Ether 1:41).

75. See the note on "faith" in verse 8.

76. This formula comes, famously, out of the gospels, where it appears five times—in Matthew 9:22; Mark 5:34; 10:52; Luke 8:48; 17:19. In the Markan and Lukan texts, the formula appears alongside a command to "go," but not to "go to" or to "go to it." In Mark 5:34 and Luke 8:48, one finds "go in peace." In Mark 10:52 and Luke 17:19, one finds "go thy way." It should be noted that Enos will use the word "whole" again in the next verse.

77. See the note on "it came to pass" in verse 1.

78. See the note on "words" in verse 3. It should be noted that the phrase "had heard these words" appears again in verse 11.

79. Enos will again use the word "began" in verse 11— "my faith began to be unshaken in the Lord." The word appears also in verse 25 in a rather different context.

80. Nowhere else in scripture is it said that desire is something felt. Moreover, even the phrase "a desire," with the indefinite article, is quite rare. It appears only four times in the Bible (in Deuteronomy 21:11; Job 14:15; Jeremiah 44:14; and Philippians 1:23). And beyond Enos, it appears just once in the Book of Mormon (in Alma 60:27). Enos never elsewhere uses the verb "to feel," but he does speak of "desires" and of "desire" in verses 12 and 13.

81. Three other passages in scripture—all of them in the Book of Mormon—speak of desire for someone's welfare. Two of them come from Jacob (in 2 Nephi 6:3 and Jacob 2:3). The other comes in Alma 60:9, the words of Moroni. Beyond this formula, the word "welfare" appears some seventeen other times in the Book of Mormon (and seven in the Old Testament).

82. This is Enos's first use of the word "brethren," but it appears again (twice) in verse 10 (in response to this desire), and then once more in verse 11 (in a parallel expression of desire).

the Nephites[83]; wherefore,[84] I did pour out my whole[85] soul[86] unto God[87] for them. **10** And while I was thus[88] struggling[89] in the Spirit,[90] behold,[91] the voice[92] of the Lord[93] came into my mind[94] again, saying, "I will visit[95]

---

83. Generally, the formula "[one's] brethren, the Nephites," is spoken in the Book of Mormon by (or in connection with the mind) of a Lamanite—as in Alma 24:7, 8; 27:5; 3 Nephi 2:12. The only other exception is Alma 37:10. Enos will refer to the Nephites as "my people, the Nephites" in verse 13 (twice), and then simply as "the Nephites" in verse 23. It should be noted that Enos uses the formula "my brethren, the Lamanites," in verse 11, and it appears in some form or another some twenty times in the Book of Mormon—although, interestingly, it does not appear before Enos's writings.

84. See the note on "wherefore" in verse 6.

85. See the note on "whole" in verse 8.

86. See the note on "soul" in verse 4. The phrase "pour out [one's] soul" is biblical, appearing five times in the Old Testament (see 1 Samuel 1:15; Job 30:16; Psalms 42:4; Isaiah 53:12; Lamentations 2:12)—only one of these passages clearly referring to prayer, however (1 Samuel 1:15). It shows up, then, some nine times in the Book of Mormon beyond Enos, all of them only after Enos. See Mosiah 14:12; 26:14; Alma 19:14; 34:26; 46:17; 58:10; Helaman 7:11, 14; Mormon 3:12. In most of these instances, prayer is at issue. Only one of these passages also uses the word "whole" to qualify "soul"—Mosiah 26:14. It is perhaps worth noting that Jacob's only use of "to pour" inverts Enos's formula: "the Lord God poured in his Spirit into my soul" (Jacob 7:8).

87. See the note on "Lord" in verse 1.

88. Somewhat surprisingly, this formula, "while [someone] was thus [doing something]," appears nowhere in the Bible, and only three times in the Book of Mormon. See, in addition to this passage in Enos, Alma 19:28; 3 Nephi 11:3.

89. This is the first use of the word "struggling" in Enos (a word that appears just ten times in the Book of Mormon), but he will use it twice more, in verse 11 and in verse 14. For other Book of Mormon uses, see Mosiah 7:18 (twice); Alma 27:1; Mormon 2:14; 5:2; 6:6; Ether 15:31.

90. Nowhere else does anyone "struggle in the Spirit." The more common formula is, of course, that the Spirit strives (or ceases to strive) with human beings; see Genesis 6:3; 1 Nephi 7:14; 2 Nephi 26:11; Mormon 5:16; Ether 2:15; 15:19; Moroni 8:26; 9:4. This verse also marks, it might be noted, Enos's sole reference to the Spirit by any title.

91. See the note on "behold" in verse 1.

92. See the note on "voice" in verse 4.

93. See the note on "Lord" in verse 1.

94. Nowhere else in scripture does a voice come into one's "mind." In fact, nowhere else in the Book of Mormon does anything at all come into one's mind. Ideas and the like, however, do come into one's mind in the Old Testament, where such a formula appears some nine times, always in the prophets (see Isaiah 65:17; Jeremiah 19:5; 32:35; 44:21; 51:50; Ezekiel 11:5; 20:32; 38:10; Daniel 2:29). This verse marks Enos's only use of the word "mind."

95. Enos only uses "visit" in this verse, though he uses it once more within the verse. It might be noted that this verb is often negative in the Book of Mormon (as, for instance, in 1 Nephi 13:33, 34; 2 Nephi 1:12, 18; 20:3; 26:6; 27:2; 28:16; Jacob 2:33; Omni 1:7—to take just examples from the small plates). It is, of course, sometimes positive as well—as in 1 Nephi 2:16; 2 Nephi 4:26. One passage in the small plates directly explores the two possible meanings of visitation side by side; see 1 Nephi 19:11.

thy brethren[96] according[97] to their diligence[98] in keeping my commandments.[99] I have given unto them this land,[100] and it is a holy land,[101] and
I curse it[102] not save it be[103] for the cause of iniquity.[104] Wherefore,[105] I
will visit[106] thy brethren[107] according[108] as[109] I have said, and their trans-

---

96. See the note on "brethren" in verse 9.

97. Enos refers back to this "according to" later in this same verse ("according as I have said").
Other formulas associated with "according to" in Enos come in verse 12 ("according to thy desires"), verse 17 ("according to the covenant"), verse 18 ("according to their faith"), and verse 26
("according to the truth").

98. The phrase "according to . . . diligence" appears four times elsewhere, always within the
Book of Mormon, and almost exclusively with reference to the Liahona. See 1 Nephi 16:28, 29;
Mosiah 1:16; Alma 12:9. Enos will refer to diligence again in verse 12 and in verse 20. The word
"diligence" (and its variants) appears frequently in scripture, but it is a particular favorite, it seems,
of Enos's father, Jacob. See 2 Nephi 6:3; 9:51; Jacob 1:7, 19; 2:3; 4:3; 5:61, 74, 75; 6:3; 7:3

99. This formula, "diligence in keeping my commandments," echoes a Deuteronomic formula
(see Deuteronomy 6:17; 11:22). It also appears another nine times in the Book of Mormon (see 1
Nephi 4:34; 15:11; 16:4; Mosiah 1:11; 4:6; 7:23; 37:20; 39:1; 3 Nephi 6:14). Interestingly, this is Enos's
only reference to keeping commandments, and even just to commandments at all.

100. The coupling of "to give" with "this land" is frequent in the Old Testament, where it always
has reference to the donation of the land of Palestine to Israel as a people (see Genesis 12:7; 15:7,
18; 24:7; 48:4; Exodus 32:13; numbers 14:8; 32:5; Deuteronomy 3:18; 26:9; Joshua 1:13; 2 Chronicles
20:7; Jeremiah 32:22). It appears elsewhere in the Book of Mormon only in Third Nephi, where
Christ, by the Father's command, gives the New-World promised land to the remnant of Jacob
(see 3 Nephi 16:16; 20:14; 21:22).

101. The phrase "holy land" appears just three times in scripture, including the present verse.
It appears just once in the Bible, in Zechariah 2:21, with reference to Judah's lands. And then it
appears in the Doctrine and Covenants, but in a passage that concerns the Book of Mormon—see
D&C 84:59. It never appears again in the Book of Mormon.

102. Lands are not cursed in the Bible. Curses come on the land (see Deuteronomy 29:27),
and lands can become a curse (see Jeremiah 44:22), but it is only in the Book of Mormon that
the land is cursed itself. In the Book of Mormon, though, this occurs with some frequency (see
1 Nephi 17:35, 38; 2 Nephi 1:7; Jacob 2:29; 3:3; Alma 37:28; 45:16; Helaman 13:18, 19, 30, 35, 36;
Mormon 1:17, 18). Enos never speaks elsewhere of a curse at all.

103. Enos twice more uses this formula, except in the indicative case ("save it was"), in verses
20 and 23. It is extremely frequent in the Book of Mormon, although it appears just once in the
Bible (1 Corinthians 1:18). It might be noted that Enos's phrasing here is strikingly similar to that
of 2 Nephi 1:31 ("save it shall be iniquity among them").

104. The phrase "the cause of iniquity" is unique to this verse. It marks, moreover, the only
times Enos uses the word "cause" or the word "iniquity."

105. See the note on "wherefore" in verse 6.

106. See the note on "visit" earlier in this same verse.

107. See the note on "brethren" in verse 9.

108. See the note on "according" earlier in this same verse.

109. The phrasing "according as" is surprisingly frequent in scripture, appearing more than
thirty times in the Bible and some twenty-one times in the Book of Mormon.

gressions[110] will I bring down with sorrow[111] upon their own heads."[112] //
11 And after that[113] I, Enos,[114] had heard these words,[115] my faith[116] began[117]
to be unshaken[118] in the Lord.[119] And I prayed[120] unto him with many
long strugglings[121] for my brethren,[122] the Lamanites.[123] **12** And it came

---

110. Enos will use the word "transgressions" again in verse 13.

111. The phrase "bring down with sorrow" clearly echoes the late patriarchal narratives. Jacob warns his sons that their actions might "bring down [his] gray hairs with sorrow to the grave" (Genesis 42:38). Judah later repeats Jacob's claim to Joseph (see Genesis 44:29, 31). Nephi then alludes to these passages in 1 Nephi 18:18 in telling a story about his own patriarchal father. Two other passages connect the same phrasing to Lehi; see 1 Nephi 16:25; 2 Nephi 1:21. All instances of the formula are thus about patriarchal figures except this one in Enos. Enos never mentions sorrow elsewhere.

112. Only one other passage in scripture uses this formulaic language of "bringing something down on someone's head." Amulek, in Alma 10:18, tells his hearers that they will "bring down the wrath of God upon [their] heads." The only other mention of heads in Enos's book is in verse 20, where he refers to the Lamanites' heads as "shaven."

113. The phrase "after that" was changed to simply "after" for the 1837 edition, and it has read that way in all subsequent printed editions.

114. See the note on "I, Enos" in verse 1.

115. See the note on "words" in verse 3, as well as the note on "had heard these words" in verse 9.

116. See the note on "faith" in verse 8.

117. See the note on "began" in verse 9.

118. The word "unshaken" appears in scripture just four times (including this passage), and only in the Book of Mormon. Twice it appears elsewhere in the small plates, and both of these—like this passage—connect the word with faith. Nephi speaks of coming to baptism "with unshaken faith" in Christ (2 Nephi 31:19), and Jacob speaks of obtaining a hope when "faith becometh unshaken" (Jacob 4:6). The only other instance of the word, in Moroni's writings, recommends asking for miracles "with a firmness unshaken" (Mormon 9:28).

119. The phrase "faith . . . in the Lord" is actually quite rare, appearing just here and in Ephesians 1:15. Far more common, however, is "trust . . . in the Lord," which appears thirty times in the Old Testament (most heavily concentrated in the poetic writings), just twice in the New Testament, and three times in the Book of Mormon (see Mosiah 4:6; 10:19; Alma 17:13). See also the note on "Lord" in verse 1.

120. See the note on "mighty prayer" in verse 4.

121. Although the printer's manuscript reads "struggleings," the 1830 typesetter set the word as "struggles." This was corrected in the 1837 edition to "strugglings," and it has appeared this way since. This is the only passage in scripture to use "many long strugglings" or even "long strug-glings," although two other passages speak of "many strugglings (Mosiah 7:18) or "many struggles" (Alma 27:1)—both of them in the Book of Mormon. See also the note on "struggling" in verse 10.

122. See the note on "brethren" in verse 9.

123. This is Enos's first reference to the Lamanites. They will be mentioned again in verse 13 (twice) as Enos continues his prayer, in verse 16 in God's response to the prayer, in verse 20 when the Nephites "seek diligently to restore the Lamanites unto the true faith in God" (and Enos provides a degrading cultural characterization of the Lamanites), and in verse 24 when

to pass[124] that after I had prayed[125] and labored[126] with all diligence,[127] the Lord[128] said unto me,[129] "I will grant[130] unto thee according[131] to thy desires,[132] because of thy faith."[133] **13** And now, behold,[134] this was the desire[135]

---

there are "wars between the Nephites and the Lamanites." See also the note on "my brethren, the Lamanites," in verse 9.

124. See the note on "it came to pass" in verse 1.

125. See the note on "mighty prayer" in verse 4.

126. The coupling of prayer and labor is infrequent in scripture. Colossians 4:12 speaking of "labouring fervently . . . in prayers," and Alma 8:10 says that "Alma labored much in the spirit, wrestling with God in mighty prayer." Otherwise, it is only this passage that pairs the two. Enos uses the word "labor" just one other time, in verse 20, when he describes his own people's efforts "to restore the Lamanites unto the true faith in God."

127. The phrase "all diligence" shows up four times in the Bible—in Proverbs 4:23; 2 Corinthians 8:7; 2 Peter 1:5; Jude 1:3—but then twelve times in the Book of Mormon. It seems especially plentiful in the small plates, where fully half of its instances appear (more often than not on the lips of Enos's father, Jacob); see 1 Nephi 10:2; 16:4; 2 Nephi 6:3; Jacob 1:19; 5:74. (Its later instances in the Book of Mormon are found in Mosiah 7:33; 26:38; Alma 21:23; 51:9; 3 Nephi 5:3; 6:14. See also the note on "diligence" in verse 10.

128. See the note on "Lord" in verse 1.

129. Enos will use this exact phrase, "the Lord said unto me," only once more, in verse 18.

130. The word "grant" appears seventy-eight times in the Book of Mormon, but this marks its first appearance; it never shows up elsewhere in the small plates.

131. See the note on "according" in verse 10.

132. The phrase "grant unto someone according to her desires" appears only in the Book of Mormon. It appears in a theologically fraught passage in Alma 29:4, but then in a more mundane setting in Alma 62:28. Closely related is the phrase "grant unto someone that they she should do according to her desires," which appears in Mosiah 21:6; Alma 20:24. See also the note on "desire" in verse 9.

133. See the note on "because of thy faith" in verse 8.

134. See the note on "behold" in verse 1.

135. This indexical identification of a desire appears a few other times in the Book of Mormon (but in no other volume of scripture). See Mosiah 18:10, 11; Alma 47:4; 55:24. Close variations appear another five times in the Book of Mormon; see Alma 18:22; 19:6; 47:15, 16; 55:19. See also the note on "desire" in verse 9.

which I desired[136] of him: that if it should so be that[137] my people, the Nephites,[138] should fall into transgression[139] and by any means[140] be destroyed,[141] and the Lamanites[142] should not be destroyed,[143] that the

---

136. This doubling of desire ("the desire which I desired") appears in only one other passage in scripture—Luke 22:15, when Jesus expresses his interest in eating a final meal with his disciples: "With desire I have desired to eat this passive with you before I suffer."

137. Against expectations, the phrase "if it should so be that" appears only in this passage in all of scripture, although "if it shall so be that" appears once also, in 3 Nephi 26:9. Similar phrases, of course, appear in certain places—such as "even if it so be" later in this same verse; see the note on that phrase.

138. The phrase "my people, the Nephites," shows up twice in this verse, and then some eight further times in the Book of Mormon. Nephi and Jacob never use the phrase, interestingly, making Enos the first to use it. It then appears in Omni 1:2, 10; Words of Mormon 1:1; Mormon 3:1, 9; 6:1; 8:7 (twice). The pattern of appearance is clear. Enos uses it, and then two of his descendants who care for the small plates. It is then used only by Mormon and Moroni (the latter just as he takes over the record from his father). The phrase "my people" with reference to the Nephites, however, shows up with great frequency in the Book of Mormon, throughout Nephi's writings and continuing right through the book. See also the note on "my brethren, the Nephites," in verse 9.

139. The phrase "fall into transgression" is unique to the Book of Mormon, never appearing in the Bible. It never appears before Enos uses it (despite the anticipations of apostasy among the Nephites in the prophecies of Nephi and Jacob). It appears after Enos, however, some seventeen times. Jarom is the only one to use the phrase in the small plates after Enos (see Jarom 1:10). But then it appears throughout the books of Mosiah, Alma, Helaman, and Third Nephi. See Mosiah 1:13; 2:40; 7:25; 15:13; Alma 9:19, 23; 10:19; 24:30; 32:19; 44:4; 46:21, 22 (twice); Helaman 3:16; 4:26; 3 Nephi 6:5. See also the note on "transgressions" in verse 10.

140. The phrase "by any means" appears in the Old Testament twice (see 1 Kings 20:39; Psalms 49:7) and in the New Testament ten times (see Luke 10:19; Acts 27:12; Romans 1:10; 11:14; 1 Corinthians 8:9; 9:27; 2 Corinthians 11:3; Galatians 2:2; Philippians 3:11; 2 Thessalonians 2:3). The instances of the phrase in the Bible seem to make it particularly (but not exclusively) Pauline. It appears some nine times, including the present passage. Nephi uses it in a related passage in 2 Nephi 5:14—the only other place where the phrase is connected to the verb "to destroy." Enos's father, Jacob, uses it twice, in Jacob 1:7; 4:18. It then appears in Mosiah 9:11; Alma 43:25; 58:9; Helaman 15:9; 3 Nephi 1:7.

141. The Book of Mormon speaks often of destruction, using the verb "to destroy" or the noun "destruction" more than four hundred and fifty times. Enos uses the verb twice in the present verse, then in verse 14 (with reference to the sacred records of the Nephites), and then in verse 20 (with reference to the Lamanites' desire to destroy the Nephites). He uses the noun in verse 23 twice, first with reference to the destructions he and other prophets have to preach to keep his people in line, and then with reference to the destruction the people actually avoid through the prophets' preaching.

142. See the note on "the Lamanites" in verse 11.

143. See the note on "destroyed" earlier in this same verse.

Lord God[144] would preserve[145] a record[146] of my people, the Nephites[147]—even if it so[148] be by the power[149] of his holy arm[150]—that it might be brought forth[151] some future day[152] unto the Lamanites,[153] that per-

---

144. This is the first instance of "Lord God" in Enos. It will appear again just in verse 15. See also the note on "Lord" in verse 1.

145. Enos uses the verb "preserve" three times, always with reference to God's preserving of the records. See verses 15 and 16 for the other references.

146. The Bible does not often speak of records. It refers to recording a handful of times, and it uses the phrase "to bear record" in the New Testament in the Johannine literature (and a few times elsewhere), but it refers to literal (and even metaphorical) records just fourteen times, mostly in the Johannine literature. The Book of Mormon, by contrast, is obsessed with records, where the noun and the verb appear around with many times more frequency. This verse marks Enos's first use of the term, but it appears again in verses 14, 15, 16, and 20 (this last in the formula "bear record"). The longer formula "record of my people" appears only here and in 1 Nephi 19:1, however (although see Mosiah 8:5). The idea of preserving a record is also relatively infrequent, mostly confined to Enos's prayer here (see verses 15 and 16), but see also Mosiah 12:8; 28:20.

147. See the note on "my brethren, the Nephites," in verse 9, and the note on "my people, the Nephites," earlier in the present verse.

148. The phrase "even if it so be" appears just three other times in scripture, all in the Book of Mormon—and in fact all in the writings of Nephi. All three other instances of the formula, in fact, appear in just one sort of context. It appears first, twice, in 1 Nephi 22:17, both times introducing the possibility that the righteous will be "preserved" or "saved," specifically "by fire." It then appears in 2 Nephi 30:10 where exactly the same claim is being made, except that the verb in question—again, "by fire"—although the verb is now "to spare." It seems important that here in Enos, the formula too concerns preservation, although of a record rather than of a people, and there is no talk of fire—instead, there is talk only of "power." The shorter formula "if it so be" appears much more frequently, still never in the Bible, but thirty-seven times in the Book of Mormon.

149. The phrase "power of his arm" is unique to the Book of Mormon (although see Daniel 11:6), where it appears three other times in some form (although "power of his holy arm" is entirely unique to this passage). Jacob uses it twice—in Jacob 2:25 and Jacob 7:24. And then it appears in Omni—in Omni 1:13. The word "power" is set in parallel with "arm" in a handful of passages in the Old Testament (but never in the Book of Mormon); see Deuteronomy 9:29; 2 Kings 17:36; Jeremiah 27:5; 32:17. It might be noted that Enos twice more refers to power, in verses 23 and 26.

150. The phrase "holy arm" originates in the Old Testament, although it appears there just twice—in Psalms 98:1 and then in Isaiah 52:10, which of course gets quoted in the Book of Mormon in Mosiah 12:24; 15:31; 3 Nephi 16:20; 20:35. It otherwise does not appear in ancient scripture, suggesting that Enos is borrowing the image from Isaiah (or perhaps from the psalm).

151. The 1830 typesetter added the word "at" after "forth," and every printed edition has retained the added preposition. It is missing, however, in both the original and the printer's manuscripts, both extant for this verse.

152. The phrase "some future day" appears elsewhere only in Moroni 1:4, where it also concerns a record coming forth to the Lamanites. There are no instances of "future day" without the prefacing "some," it might be noted.

153. See the note on "the Lamanites" in verse 11.

haps[154] they might be brought unto salvation.[155] **14** (For at the present[156] our strugglings[157] were vain[158] in restoring[159] them to the true faith,[160] and they swore in their wrath[161] that, if it were possible,[162] they would destroy[163] our records[164] and us, and also all[165] the traditions of our fathers.)[166]

---

154. This is Enos's only use of the word "perhaps," but it might be noted that the word is far less frequent in scripture than might be guessed. It appears just three times in the Bible, always in the New Testament, and then only forty-three times in the Book of Mormon. It is worth pointing out that it appears rather frequently, given its general infrequency, in Jacob's writings, but always and only within the allegory of the olive tree (where it appears eight times; see Jacob 5:4, 11, 27, 53, 54, 59, 60 [twice]).

155. Only one other passage speaks of "bringing someone unto salvation"—2 Nephi 3:15, quoting Joseph of Egypt. Generally, instead, scripture speaks of "bringing salvation unto someone"—a formula that appears twice in Third Isaiah (see Isaiah 59:16; 63:5), and then four times in the Book of Mormon (see 2 Nephi 2:3; 29:4; Alma 34:15; 3 Nephi 18:32).

156. This is the only instance of the phrase "at the present" in all of scripture.

157. See the note on "struggling" in verse 10.

158. Scripture of course speaks often of vanity, but it might be noted that two other passages couple struggling with vanity. See Mosiah 7:18; Alma 27:1.

159. Only Enos speaks of restoring anyone to a "faith," and he does it here and in verse 20. Enos's father, Jacob, speaks of restoring Jews "to the truth church and fold of God" (2 Nephi 9:2), of Nephites being restored "that they may come to that which will give them the true knowledge of their Redeemer" (2 Nephi 10:2), and of restoring Lamanites "to the knowledge of the truth" (Jacob 7:24)—all these are obviously related to Enos's phrasing here.

160. Enos provides two of scripture's four references to a "true faith," here and in verse 20. The phrase shows up also in Alma 44:4; 3 Nephi 6:14. It might be noted that the phrase always responds to *a* or *the* true faith, never to one's faith or belief being true. See also the note on "faith" in verse 8.

161. The formula "swear in one's wrath" appears in Psalms 95:11, which is then quoted in Hebrews 3:11 and Hebrews 4:3, as well as in Jacob 1:7 and Alma 12:35. It appears in non-psalmic contexts only in the Book of Mormon, where it appears in Mosiah 19:4; Ether 1:33; 2:8; 15:28. Twice elsewhere is someone described as being wroth and then swearing—in Deuteronomy 1:34 and Alma 49:27. This passage constitutes Enos's only reference to swearing or wrath.

162. The phrase "if it were possible" shows up frequently enough elsewhere in scripture (although it never appears in the Old Testament—where even the word "possible" alone never shows up). This is Enos's only reference to possibility by this term.

163. See the note on "destroyed" in verse 13.

164. See the note on "record" in verse 13.

165. This is the only passage in scripture where "traditions" (whether "of our fathers" or not) is qualified by "all."

166. The phrase "traditions of our fathers" (with "our" or another possessive pronoun) appears just once in the Bible, when Paul refers to the traditions of his fathers, for which he was zealous (see Galatians 1:14). It shows up, however, some twenty-seven times in the Book of Mormon. This passage marks its first instance in the Book of Mormon, and it never appears elsewhere in the small plates. (The word "tradition" pure and simple appears only here in all of the small plates, in fact.) Within the Book of Mormon, it appears most often in Alma (seventeen times), but it also

15 Wherefore,[167] I, knowing[168] that the Lord God[169] was able[170] to preserve[171] our records,[172] I cried[173] unto him continually[174]—for he had said
unto me, "Whatsoever thing[175] ye shall ask in faith,[176] believing that ye
shall receive[177] in the name[178] of Christ,[179] ye shall receive it." **16** And I

---

appears in Mosiah (three times), Helaman (five times), and Third Nephi (just once). As here, it
sometimes refers to the traditions of specifically Nephite fathers (in Mosiah 26:1; Alma 9:8; 30:14,
16, 23, 27, 31; 3 Nephi 1:11), but it most often refers to the traditions of the Lamanites' fathers. See
also the note on "father" in verse 1.

167. See the note on "wherefore" in verse 6.

168. See the note on "knowing" in verse 1.

169. See the note on "Lord God" in verse 13 and the note on "Lord" in verse 1.

170. The word "able" appears with astonishing infrequency in the Book of Mormon—just
seventeen times, and only here in the Book of Enos. Its other uses in the small plates appear in
1 Nephi 4:3; 7:12; 11:1; 16:1; 2 Nephi 27:20, 21; Jacob 4:9 (twice). In the small plates, with only
one exception (see 1 Nephi 16:1), the word is only used to describe God. Striking, after the small
plates, with only one exception (see Ether 3:5), the word is only used to describe human beings.

171. See the note on "preserve" in verse 13.

172. See the note on "record" in verse 13.

173. See the note on "cried" in verse 4.

174. Enos will use the word "continually" three more times in his short book—in verses 20
and 23 (twice in the latter)—with reference to Lamanite efforts to destroy the Nephites, and with
reference to the consistent efforts of Nephite prophets to bring their people to repentance. The
only other passage in scripture where "continually" is coupled with the verb "to cry" is Mosiah
21:11, where it concerns the cries of widows for vengeance.

175. The phrase "whatsoever thing" (or its slight variant "what thing soever") appears sixteen
times in the Bible, and then twenty-three times in the Book of Mormon. It occurs in a larger
formula about asking and faith, however, only in a few places. See Mark 11:24; 3 Nephi 27:28;
Mormon 9:27; Moroni 7:26. Enos will use the word "thing" again in the singular in verse 18, with
an apparent echo of this verse.

176. The phrase "ask in faith" appears just once in the Bible (see James 1:6), and then only
here in the Book of Mormon, although "ask me in faith" appears in 1 Nephi 15:11, and "ask . . .
in faith" appears in Mosiah 4:21 and Moroni 7:26"—all three of these other passages followed by
the same "believing . . ." clause that appears here. See also, though, the note on "faith" in verse 8.

177. The qualifying clause "believing that ye shall receive" appears five other times in the
Book of Mormon, always in similar contexts (it never appears in the Bible); see 1 Nephi 15:11;
Mosiah 4:21; Alma 22:16; 3 Nephi 18:20; Moroni 7:26. This is the only reference to belief in Enos.

178. See the note on "name" in verse 1.

179. The phrase "name of Christ" appears only twice in the New Testament (in 2 Timothy
2:19; 1 Peter 4:14) but twenty-three times in the Book of Mormon. It appears several times in
the closing chapters of Second Nephi (see 2 Nephi 31:13; 32:9; 33:12), but otherwise only here in
the small plates. It then appears scattered throughout the rest of the Book of Mormon. Only in two
other passages is "the name of Christ" attached to the verb "to ask"—by passages written by Moroni
(see Mormon 9:21; Moroni 10:4). See also the notes on "Lord" in verse 1 and "Christ" in verse 8.

had faith.[180] And I did cry[181] unto God[182] that he would preserve[183] the records,[184] and he covenanted[185] with me that he would bring them forth unto the Lamanites[186] in his own due time.[187] **17** And I, Enos,[188] knew[189] that[190] it would be according[191] to the covenant[192] which he had made; wherefore,[193] my soul[194] did rest.[195]

---

180. See the note on "faith" in verse 8.

181. See the note on "cried" in verse 4.

182. On the title "God," see the note on "Lord" in verse 1.

183. See the note on "preserve" in verse 16.

184. See the note on "record" in verse 13.

185. Covenants are often mentioned in the small plates—and throughout the Book of Mormon. Enos uses the word here and in verse 17—at that point with direct reference back to this covenant here.

186. See the note on "the Lamanites" in verse 11.

187. The phrase "his own due time" (or variations using a different opening possessive pronoun) is unique to the Book of Mormon. It appears before this point only in 2 Nephi 27:21, where it also concerns the coming forth of records. After Enos, it does not appear again until 3 Nephi 5:25, where it concerns the restoration of the house of Jacob, and 3 Nephi 20:29, where it concerns the gathering. It appears again in Mormon 5:12 with respect to the coming forth of records. Finally, it appears in Ether 3:24, 27, where it concerns the translatability of the sealed portion (which is the record to come forth in 2 Nephi 27:21 as well). Related to this phrase, obviously, is "the own due time of the Lord," which appears three times as well—all in Nephi's writings. In 1 Nephi 10:3, this phrase appears in connection with the return of Jews from Babylonian exile. In 1 Nephi 14:26, it concerns sealed and written records coming forth once more, as it does one last time in 2 Nephi 27:10.

188. See the note on "I, Enos" in verse 1.

189. See the note on "knew" in verse 6.

190. The word "that" appears in the printer's manuscript, but it was dropped by the 1830 typesetter, and it has never appeared in any printed edition. The original manuscript is not extant for this verse.

191. See the note on "according" in verse 10.

192. See the note on "covenanted" in verse 16.

193. See the note on "wherefore" in verse 6.

194. See the note on "soul" in verse 4.

195. Souls rest just a few times in the Bible. Psalms 116:7 finds the psalmist commanding his soul to "return" to its "rest." In Jeremiah 6:16 is a promise to "find rest for your souls." And Matthew 11:29 famously promises to those take up Christ's yoke that they will "find rest unto your souls." In the Book of Mormon, this connection appears just three times outside of Enos. Alma 37:34 promises to the meek and lowly that they "shall find rest to their souls." Alma 57:36 expresses trust that the righteous slain's souls "have entered into the rest of their God." And Moroni 9:6 finds Mormon hoping that he and his son will "rest our souls in the kingdom of God." No passage in ancient scripture quite approaches the simple formula Enos uses. It should be noted that Enos will twice more use "rest" in verse 27: "And I soon go to the place of my rest, which is with my Redeemer; for I know that in him I shall rest."

18 And the Lord[196] said unto me,[197] "Thy fathers[198] have also required[199] of me this thing,[200] and it shall be done[201] unto them according[202] to their faith[203]—for their faith[204] was like[205] unto thine."

---

196. See the note on "Lord" in verse 1.

197. See the note on "the Lord said unto me" in verse 12.

198. See also the note on "father" in verse 1.

199. The word "require" is actually rather rare in the Book of Mormon. It appears before this point only in 1 Nephi 3:5, where it appears twice—with a question raised about who has "required of" Laman and Lemuel to return to Jerusalem for the brass plates. It then appears in Mosiah 2:22, 24, summarizing "all that [God] requires of" his servants. In Mosiah 18:27, describing the order of Alma's church, it is said that "little should be required" of those who have little to give. And Alma 34:12 says that "the law requireth the life of him who hath murdered."

200. See the note on "whatsoever thing" in verse 15.

201. The phrase "it shall be done" appears five times in the Bible, either in formal contexts or in contexts of promising a response to a request (see Esther 9:12; Obadiah 1:15; Matthew 18:19; 21:21; John 15:7). The same is true of the Book of Mormon, where it appears eight times in addition to the present passage (see 2 Nephi 3:25; Helaman 10:8, 9; 12:20; 3 Nephi 21:11; Mormon 8:15, 16; Moroni 7:26).

202. See the note on "according" in verse 10.

203. See the note on "faith" in verse 8.

204. See the note on "faith" in verse 8.

205. The only other passage in scripture where "faith" is "like" is 2 Peter 1:1, where reference is made to "like precious faith."

Made in the USA
Las Vegas, NV
26 November 2024

12685074R00095